My Journey

From Ordinary Seaman to Master Mariner

DONALD J. CRIGHTON

My Journey
Copyright © 2024 by Donald J. Crighton

All rights reserved. No part of this publication may be reproduced, distributed, or transmitted in any form or by any means, including photocopying, recording, or other electronic or mechanical methods, without the prior written permission of the author, except in the case of brief quotations embodied in critical reviews and certain other non-commercial uses permitted by copyright law.

Tellwell Talent
www.tellwell.ca

ISBN
978-1-77941-557-8 (Paperback)

TABLE OF CONTENTS

Chapter 1   CANADIAN COAST GUARD 1

                Kitsilano Base 1

                Bull Harbour 4

                Commercial Fisherman 8

Chapter 2   MV WESTERN HEMLOCK 9

Chapter 3   MV HENRY CHRISTOFFERSEN 21

Chapter 4   FISHERIES PATROL VESSELS 24

                FPC Howay 24

                FPC Tanu 25

Chapter 5   EDWARD O VETTER 29

Chapter 6   MV FORTUNE KING/MV SLEEPING BEAUTY 52

                MV Fortune King 52

                MV Sleeping Beauty 68

Chapter 7   SLEEPING BEAUTY 2 87

Chapter 8   MV BERNIER 104

Chapter 9   M.V. BERNIER 2 115

Chapter 10   MV BERNIER 3 125

Chapter 11   MV PROBE RESEARCHER 138

Chapter 12   PROBE RESEARCHER 2 148

Chapter 13   BC FERRY CORPORATION 155

Prologue 161

Appendix A 168

CHAPTER 1

CANADIAN COAST GUARD

My first sea going career actually started with the Canadian Coast Guard. Most of my time was spent at the Kitsilano Base at False Creek in Vancouver working as a seamen on what were called crash boats. These were left over WW2 air force search and rescue craft originally stationed at the air force base at Jericho in Vancouver, used I am guessing, to rescue downed fliers. I would work either the day shift or the night shift basically waiting for a call to assist someone in distress in the English Bay area. The Coast Guard also stationed two lifeboats, one on the west coast at Bamfield and another at Bull Harbour on Hope Island off the northern tip of Vancouver Island. They also had three 90 foot cutters, the Racer, the Ready, and the Rider. These were live aboard boats assigned to patrol the waters of the West Coast, the Gulf Islands or the North Coast. The Gulf Island patrol area was also known as the pub patrol. I worked mainly out of the base at Kitsilano but was often sent to the lifeboat at Bull Harbour or to a one of the cutters.

Kitsilano Base

When assigned to Kitsilano there was a crew of four on duty 24 hours a day. A coxswain and three seamen. If we were called out on a rescue one of the seaman, called a peggy, was detailed to stay behind and answer the phones. On one occasion we were all sitting around the lounge watching a hockey game when we got a call that there was a jumper on the Burrard Street bridge, literally within spitting distance of our dock. Before working for the Coast Guard I had no idea how many people committed suicide, or attempted suicide, by jumping off of one of Vancouver's bridges. On that night I was fairly new to this business, I was also the peggy for the night. Because we were so close to the bridge, only about a boat length away, I was standing on our dock watching the action unfold. There were the usual gathering of emergency vehicles on the bridge, lots of flashing lights, firemen, police and such. Our crash boat, the Mallard or the Moorhen, was stationed under the bridge to rescue the individual or recover the body. The crew on board the boat were older than I was and had worked there for years. They had seen this situation many times, they also wanted to get back to their hockey game. While the gang up on the bridge were trying to talk the individual out of jumping, the boat crew down below were shouting, "jump jump". I guess they were anxious to get the situation resolved and return to the hockey game. The firemen on the bridge did finally manage to talk the the individual out of jumping.

Another time, while out on patrol in the crash boat somewhere in English Bay we came across a small yacht that had broken down. I don't recall what his problem was but we were able to fix the issue and send him on his way. As we were untying from his boat he offered us a case of beer. The coxswain said sorry no we are not allowed to accept anything especially liquor. Well, the grateful boat owner was not going to accept no for an answer. As the coxswain was pulling away and the gap between the boats started to widen he opened the case of beer and started throwing the bottles to me one at a time. The crash boat was made from steel and if I didn't catch these bottles they would shatter on our decks and maybe shower us with broken glass, a very dangerous situation. I had no choice, I had to catch them. I caught all 12 bottles!

I was also occasionally assigned to one of the cutters. These three boats were live aboards, two weeks on and two weeks off, and assigned to one of three patrol areas, The West Coast of Vancouver Island, the East side of Vancouver Island, or North of Vancouver Island. When it was time for a crew change, the cutter in question would come in and lay along side our pier at Kits base. This crew change would take a day or two depending on how much in the way of stores had to be put on board or if any repairs were needed. One evening while alongside I came up to the wheel house for my evening watch where I found two of the crew intently staring, with binoculars, at a high rise apartment on the other side of False Creek across the way from Kits Base. It turns out that there was a lady in one apartment who had a habit of removing her clothing in front of her window. One of the seaman engaged in this peeping tom exercise was known as somewhat of a ladies man. His exploits with the ladies were apparently legendary. It was said he could get a date in the middle of the Atlantic Ocean. Well Mr. Casanova was determined to meet this lady, so a plan was hatched. Looking into her apartment window you could see the intercom on the wall opposite the window. The plan was for Mr. Casanova to take a rubber boat and a hand held radio across to the other side of False Creek and make his way up to the main entrance of the apartment building. We knew what floor she lived but not her apartment number. So lover boy would ring each apartment on the twelve floor in sequence while his partner in crime would watch from the cutter's wheel house. He would radio over to the cutter, "I am pushing the buzzer for apartment 1201". The watcher would then radio back,"nothing on 1201". And so it went. When the watcher saw our lady friend pick up her in-house phone he knew they had the correct apartment. It worked and Mr Casanova did get to date the girl.

Another time aboard one of the cutters we were again tied up at the Kitsilano base for a couple of days. It was also Christmas eve. One of the other seaman lived on Bowen Island. He was missing his family and it being Christmas Eve, the captain agreed to let him take the rubber boat and a radio and head for home for the night. The plan was, in the event we got a call out, we would radio the seaman and pick him up when we passed Bowen Island. Being a conscientious sailor, he placed the radio under his coat and foul weather gear to protect it from spray. What he didn't know was that by doing so he had inadvertently pressed and held the talk button. What we heard on the cutters bridge was him noisily smoking a joint and merrily singing Jingle Bells. There was no way we could alert him as to the situation. You cannot receive an incoming transmission with the transmit button pressed.

Bull Harbour

I also spent some time working on the lifeboat out of Bull Harbour on Hope Island just off the northern tip of Vancouver Island. Most of the people that worked out of Kit's Base hated the idea of spending two weeks cooped up in the coast guard house at Bull Harbour, a long way from the bright lights. I was the exception, as I loved every minute of my two-week shift. The coxswain I worked under was a British sailor who had served in the Royal Navy during WW2. He had survived several sinkings during the war, a few where he was among only a handful of survivors. He was also an ex-commercial salmon fisherman. He had rigged the lifeboat with trolling gear, so while on patrol we also fished for salmon. One of the other seaman I worked with at this time was an indigenous guy, named Bill George or something like that. He had a wonderful sense of humour, you never knew what to expect with him. When I first met him he told me his name and then said, "never trust a man with two first names". The house we lived in at Bull Harbour was about a mile from where the lifeboat was docked. Every morning we would hike down to the boat for a day of painting or heading out on patrol. One morning on our walk down to the boat he leaped out in front of us and held his hands up signalling for us stop. I was thinking what is he doing has he spotted a bear or something. He then proceeded to lie flat on his belly on the road with his ear pressed to the ground. What is going on? He then leaps up and in a fake lisping voice says, "white man two maybe three days", and then promptly resumes the walk to the boat.

It wasn't always fun and fishing though. We did tow in our fair share of disabled salmon trollers, but that was usually out and back in good weather, a round trip of maybe a 2 hours, at the most. Then one night we got a call for a tuna fisherman disabled 50 miles west of Triangle Island. The waters off Triangle Island are notorious for big waves, the biggest ever recorded in this area was over 100 feet, and here we were headed out in a full gale of 50 to 60 knots of wind at night. We struggled for several hours out to his position in mountainous seas, our gallant little ship more a submarine than a ship. By little ship I mean little, these lifeboats were all of 40 feet long. They were also self righting which meant if we rolled over we would roll back, or so the theory goes. And roll they did.

It was said these boats would roll on a wet lawn. The pilot house was fitted with some special seats that you strapped yourself into almost like a fighter pilot. Even though we were strapped in our stomachs were not. After about 4 or 5 hours we finally spotted our disabled tuna boat, or should I say ship. It was at least 3 times our size at around 120 feet, and at some point on the way out I can recall the coxswain commenting whether or not this guy knows what sort of ship or boat is coming to his rescue. Having located him, the next challenge was to get a tow line across to him. These lifeboats were designed with a well deck amidships. There was the pilot house forward and a compartment aft for the people we had rescued. Separating these was the well deck. Standing in this well deck you are right at the water level, making it easier for any rescue attempts. That is in calm seas. In our situation with the huge mountainous seas this deck was under water more than it was above. There was only 3 of us on board, the coxswain and 2 seamen. We were tied to the lifeboat with safety harnesses and life lines but that didn't stop us from getting soaked to the skin. Somehow we managed to get a tow line aboard the casualty. To this day I don't know how we managed that feat. One minute we were looking up at the tuna boat towering 3 stories above our heads and the next we were looking 3 stories down on him. I can only chalk it up to the skill of the coxswain who not only managed to get us into a position to get a heaving line aboard but at the same time prevent us from crashing into him. That was the easy part. Once underway with our tow things went from bad to worse. These lifeboats had 2 engines. We had only just begun our return trip when one engine died. The coxswain tried to restart it several times without success so we soldiered on with the remaining engine. Then it died as well. These engines used an air starting system, rather than an electric starter motor. There were two pressure tanks used to store compressed air for this air start system. To keep these tanks full there is an engine driven air compressor, but only on one engine. You guessed it, the first engine to fail was the one with air compressor. So when we tried to start that engine we used up all the air in the storage tanks and even with the other engine running we were not re-filling these pressure tanks. Now we were dead in the water and if you think we were getting tossed around while under power, well that was nothing once we became a log. The boat was fitted with a hand pump situated between the two engines for emergency purposes. The first order of the day though was to find out why the engines had both stopped. The coxswain decided it was a fuel problem. He spent the next hour or so crouched, no standing head room here and very hot, over the engines bleeding and priming the fuel systems. The next order of business was to pump by hand, air into the pressure tanks. The three of us took turns manning this hand pump. It was extremely hard work requiring both hands and every muscle you had, all the while crouched on your knees between the engines and trying not to get thrown around. I calculated that for every 100 strokes of the pump handle we would increase the pressure by only one or two pounds. We needed 120 PSI. At some point I passed out. The next thing I knew I was lying on the floor of the wheelhouse and we were underway again with both engines running. I still don't know how long I was out for, or how I got out of the engine room. We finally got back to Bull Harbour around 18 hours after we departed. We were used to the fishermen we towed in giving us some small token of their appreciation for our efforts, mostly a salmon or small halibut but on one occasion some fresh baked cookies from the fisherman's wife. After we had secured the tuna boat alongside, her captain said he had something for us. We were expecting some tuna. What we got was some well worn and stained, I like to think they were water stains, pornographic magazines. Thanks but no thanks.

Commercial Fisherman

After a couple of years with the coast guard, I purchased my first commercial fishing vessel from the coxswain I worked with and started on the next chapter in my life.

CHAPTER 2

MV WESTERN HEMLOCK

I GUESS MY STORY SHOULD START with the MV (motor vessel) Western Hemlock. She was a small, 10,000 ton Ro-Ro/tanker belonging to a company out of Vancouver BC, "Maple Leaf Shipping". They owned or managed two ships, the Douglas Fir and my ship the, Western Hemlock. The ink was not quite dry on my third mates certificate when I decided that this was the ship for me. I'm not quit sure how I came that decision, maybe because it was a Vancouver company and close to home. At that time there was very little in the way of oceangoing opportunities for a Canadian. Also, around that time the only chance of a sea going career locally was with coastal tugs or BC Ferries, both of which I applied for without success. The tug boat business was somewhat of a closed shop, you had to know or be related to someone. BC Ferries would give me a job as a parking lot attendant with the opportunity to get a few hours a month on board one of their ships should someone call in sick. That was definitely not in my game plan, I was on the move, as it were, and spending my days in a parking lot was not going to get me where I wanted to be. So I set my sights on Maple Leaf Shipping. I don't know how I came to even know about MLS, but this was my ticket to better things.

Maple Leaf shipping had an office in down town Vancouver. The head honcho was a man named John May. I walked into his office one day and handed over my very limited resume with a copy of my new third mate's certificate. Well that went over like a lead balloon and I was told not to let the door hit me in the rear end on my out. I still don't know why I was so persistent but I was not going to be put off so easily. I then proceeded to phone John May every morning at 9 AM for the next several months. It didn't matter if I was at home, a relatives home, or somewhere in between. Every morning at 9 AM John would get my call. Then one day my calling produced the desired results and I was told to report to Lynn Terminal in North Vancouver to join the MV Western Hemlock.

The Western Hemlock and her sister ship were designed to carry forest products, lumber or cedar shingles, to California, LA or San Fransisco, and return to BC with a load of bunker C oil which was used to power the BC pulp mills. This went on for several months, up and down the west coast, but again the writing was on the wall. The trade was drying up, we were carrying less and less down and nothing back. So one day we were ordered south through the Panama Canal and into the Caribbean. This is where the fun starts.

One of our first stops after exiting the canal was Beaumont Texas. Beaumont was situated on a river where a deep sea vessel could literally tie up in the down town core. At that time the city, as was a lot of towns and cities of that day, falling on hard times. The shopping and businesses had moved to the suburbs and the up and coming malls, all the while leaving the downtown area looking like a ghost town with lots of boarded up stores. One of the crew on board was an apprentice radio operator, Elizabeth. She was a delightful young girl, intelligent and fun to be with. However, and I don't mean to sound like I didn't care for her or that I had nothing but the highest regard for her, but she was not blessed with the looks and figure of Marilyn Monroe. Also she talked in a high squeaky voice, hence her nick name, Squeaky. I'm not sure if we called her that to her face or if she herself was the source of the name. She was, like myself, fixated on her career and looks or voice be damned, was not going to let anything or anyone to stand in her way. So one afternoon I invited her for a run ashore in downtown Beaumont. There was not a lot see except old boarded up buildings from the 30's. We finally came across a bar, about the only one open for business we had come across. So in we went. Both of us being young and naive and from Canada and not having being exposed to the racial tensions of the southern USA, we were in for a surprise. It turned out to be an African American only establishment, not that this meant a lot to us, we just wanted a beer. There were a lot of very black people, very lively, music, lots of talking and all. As soon as we walked in the noice level drop to zero, you could hear a pin drop, and of course we were now the centre of attention. So what was wrong with this picture, a white man with a skinny white chic in a crowd of black dudes who are now giving us the evil eye. We were just about to leave, at Squeaky's request, when a very large man approached and sat down at our table. If you have ever seen a Hollywood image of an African American man dressed like a pimp, or even imagined what one would look like, this was it. He was dressed in a pink suit with a frilly shirt open to his navel and a huge Panama like hat complete with ribbons and bows. And, of course, enough gold chains and ear rings to satisfy the national debt. His wardrobe also sported a pair of high heeled boots. The heels were at least 3 inches high and made from clear plastic. They were filled with water and had several small gold fishing swimming around inside. Now what do we do? He was quite friendly in a menacing sort of way, asking us where we were from and how we got here.

After a few questions he was satisfied with who we were and not some undercover cops or what ever and bought us both a beer. As soon as he signalled to the bar tender for the beer, the whole place went back to normal almost as if someone had thrown a switch. The music came back on, people started talking among themselves, and most importantly no one was giving us that "if you make one wrong move you are dead stare". After Squeaky left the ship a few months later I lost track of her until many years later when I was working for BC Ferries out of Prince Rupert. I heard her voice on the Coast Guard radio station. I tried to find her but when I finally had a chance to visit the station she was gone. They told me she had packed everything into her car and headed east.

Our next stop was San Juan, Puerto Rico. At this time the captain had his wife on board. He knew I was married and suggested I invite my wife to join us. We were due to depart San Juan in an hour or so, headed for Port of Spain in Trinidad. In those days the only way to make an international phone call was to go to the phone company's office. With little more than an hour to spare I ran through town to get to the phone office, where you hand your number to a teller like lady behind a wicker sort of window. She calculates the cost, you pay up front and are told to wait. When you are called you are directed to a phone booth where the phone had already started to ring. Louise answered the phone at work. I had little time to explain, not wanting to miss sailing with my ship. I think my words were "the captain has invited you to join the ship in Port of Spain, Trinidad, in 2 days time, Bye". I then ran as hard as I could, making it back on board just as they were pulling up the gangway.

If I think about it now, WHAT WAS I THINKING! Louise was working full time, she had no passport, how was she supposed to find me, and airline travel is not what it is today.

Cut to 2 days later and we are arriving in Port of Spain. As third officer my job, while docking, is on the bridge where I obey the pilots commands for engine movements, monitoring the VHF, and recording everything in a log called the bell book. It was around midnight and we were just coming along side when I take a call from ashore about some lady looking for the third mate. Well I guessed that must be me. Somehow in 2 days she had obtained a passport and booked a flight to Trinidad, arriving at exactly the same as I did. When she got off the plane she hailed a taxi and told the driver to take her where the ships dock. Beyond amazing!

After we took on a load of bunker C oil in Port of Spain we were bound for Port-au-Prince in Haiti. Upon arriving at Port-au-Prince we were directed to a cement plant across the bay. We tied up to a cement jetty, hooked up the discharge hose, and started pumping off, expecting to depart the next day. That was not to be. The underground pipe line to the storage tanks ashore burst, with black oil gushing out of the ground only a few meters from the jetty. Stop pumping. It took the plant workers a week to fix the pipe. In the meantime what do we do. As it happened there was an island, Isle Cacique, a short walk from the ship which just happened to host a Club Med style resort. Beautiful beaches, cold drinks, and excellent food. So for the next week the entire crew spent every waking minute sitting on the beach sipping rum punches, and eating shrimp and avocado salads, and me with Louise by my side. We all had to stand our watches, 4 hours on 8 hours off. As third officer I had the 8 to 12 watch. So from 8 in the morning until noon I stood my watch. Then from noon until 8PM was spent at the resort, then the 8 to midnight watch on board and repeat. It was a wonderful paid holiday. To get to the island you had to walk down a sandy road where you were ferried to the island in a small boat. After only a few days, rather than have us walk to catch the boat, they started picking up and dropping us off directly from the ship.

Our next port of call was Bridgetown in Barbados. This was a small ship so we only carried three seamen, one for each watch. These three deadbeats were supplied by the Seaman's International Union and they were below the bottom of the barrel. All three were ignorant, belligerent, lazy, and raving alcoholics. We had problems with them from the moment we left Vancouver. I remember watching from the bridge as they were working scaling and painting a portion of the fore deck. In a four hour watch the seaman assigned to my watch had accomplished scaling only, an area of about one square foot, no primer and no paint. This went on for a couple of days with absolutely no work being done by any of them. They didn't even have to do the scaling by hand, but instead we had a machine to do the work. I guess the chief mate had had enough and read them the riot act. Next day we found the scaling machine and all the paint had been thrown overboard. Aside from getting no work out of them they were constantly drunk. We had, as most cargo ships do, a bonded store where you could buy alcohol as well as things like toothpaste or snacks. Why the captain kept selling them the booze was beyond me. Well it all came to a head in Bridgetown. Shortly after we were secured alongside I had to report to the captain for some reason. As I approached his cabin, the door was open, and I could hear shouting. It was the three stooges. When you buy something from the bonded stores the captain notes the amount and deducts it from your pay. Also if you need cash for a run ashore you can ask the captain for an advance against your pay. As it turns out these three idiots had used up their entire pay checks, either from buying booze or a cash advances and the captain would not give them any more money. They started screaming obscenities and finally openly threatening the captain and his wife. I actually heard them threaten to kill the captain's wife. That was it, the police were called and all three were forcibly removed from the ship and taken into custody. I never found out what happened to them. All this left us in a bit of a bind though, we needed 3 new seamen or we couldn't sail. So my wife, the captain's wife, and Squeaky were pressed into service as replacement seamen. As it turned out the company had had enough as well. We were ordered to Savannah Georgia and our last trip aboard the good ship Western Hemlock.

When we arrived in Savannah we were met by a group of people, among them a company representative, a union representative, and in the case of the officers, a guild representative. I think there was a couple of lawyers thrown in for good measure. It seems the ship was to be turned over to new owners or new management, maybe both. However, there was a problem, for the officers at least. The Canadian Merchant Service Guild, a union of sorts for ships officers, although the guild did not like to use the word union, had a three year contract to supply officers, deck and engineering for Maple Leaf Shipping and the Western Hemlock. At first we were allowed to remain on board with our days spent picketing the ship. Louise, the captain's wife, Squeaky, the second officer, and a few others flew home that first day leaving only 5 or 6 of us for picket duty. I can't recall how long this went on for, a week maybe. Then a sheriff arrived to seize or impound the ship until the lawyers could sort things out. We were then sent to a hotel to spend the nights while still continuing to head back to the ship in the morning for another day of picketing. After about another week of this we got up as usual and headed down to the ship only to find it was gone. The owners had posted a bond which allowed them to take the vessel. So the rest of us flew home the next day. All the while we were in Savannah we did not know what was happening at home. It turns out we were one of the top news stories of the day. It must have a slow week for news, no wars or assignations. Vancouver sailors stranded in Savannah or something like that. When the plane landed in Vancouver a news cameraman was allowed on board before anyone could depart. I don't remember how he or the stewardesses singled us out but we were filmed walking up the aisle of the plane with the cameraman walking backwards in front of us.

So ended my first seagoing job as a third officer, which was not quite the end. About three years later I get a call from the guild to come and pick up my cheque. What cheque?? Remember that bond that was posted in order to release the ship, well after three years the lawyers had had their say and we were awarded compensation. As third officer I received $3000.00. BONUS!!

Before I leave the Western Hemlock saga behind, I have a few more unrelated situations that reveal a bit more of life on board. The first deals with my octant, but before I get into that let me explain about navigation in the 70's. At that time there was no such thing as sat-nav or GPS. There was, at least in the northern hemisphere, Loran but we did not have that luxury. To navigate up and down the west coast when close to shore, you used, mostly radar, to plot fixed points of land or lighted aids to navigation on the particular chart of the area. However, we took the offshore route, which was to head offshore for between 100 and 200 miles. There were several reasons for this. One was to avoid the inshore currents, which depending on your direction, north or south, could either hinder or aid your voyage. Another was that there was less coastal traffic to deal with. And finally the weather was more favourable. That means you have no coastal aids to navigation in order to fix your position and without satellite navigation systems to rely on, you are forced to use the age old sextant. While out at sea knowing your exact position is not too critical, but how do you know when to turn and head closer to shore for your run into San Fransisco or the straights of Juan de Fuca, without knowing where you are in the first place. Welcome to the sextant and celestial navigation. I guess the captain saw something in me similar to himself. I was very enthusiastic and really keen to learn this form of navigation, which is actually more an art than science, or maybe a bit of both leaning towards the art side. On each trip north and south he schooled me in this now almost forgotten form of navigation. Fast forward to a stop over in San Pedro (Los Angeles). On a trip ashore one day I came across an antique store. While browsing around the store I spotted a case with their most expensive items on display, the centre piece being an octant. First a little lesson about a sextant vs an octant, the arc of a sextant is the sixth part of a circle while an octant's arc is an eighth part of a circle. Both instruments must be made from a material that does not expand or contract with temperature variations in different climates or the readings obtained will not be accurate. The frame of our modern sextant on board was made from a who knows what kind of metal that met these requirements. However in the 1700's and 1800's the manufacturers of these instruments did not have these materials. The frame of the octant I came across that day was made from ebony and the scale was carved out of ivory. There was a hand written note inside the case that said the optics had been reground in 1858 by a shop in San Fransisco. So it must have dated from the early 1800's at least. I had to have it. The price, I think, was around $1200.00 USD, a princely sum when you are earning around $300.00 per month. I went back to the ship and told the captain of my discovery. He came to the shop to see for himself and he too agreed that I must have it. We went back to the ship and cleared out his safe, every last penny, and along with what I had in my pocket I was able to buy my octant. I still have it to this day. On another trip while in San Fransisco I took it by the shop whose address was on that hand written label and showed it to the shop owner. She just about fell over. She identified the hand writing as her grandfather's. I did use it at sea alongside the ships sextant and it did work just fine, maybe not as accurate as our sextant but close enough to get us where we were going.

    The second incident took place in San Pedro. The cargo area on the Western Hemlock was a large enclosed hanger like space above the main deck about the size of a football field. There were two large doors to this space, one at the stern and one on the port side forward. Outside the aft door was an open area of the main deck, like a back porch. Forklifts were craned down onto this porch in order to move the cargo in and out of the enclosed portion. To keep the forklifts from getting too close to the edge of this open deck and potentially going over the side, there was a raised metal barrier surrounding the perimeter of the deck. The side door, however did not have this protection. Instead, we had a 12 inch by 12 inch timber that we dragged into place across the opening of the door. When discharging our cargo in San Pedro they put 2 forklifts on board along with their operators and a whole host of other longshoremen. There was usually at least six other guys who did absolutely no work. One was designated as first aid attendant, but the rest I was never able to determine their roles. One day we were setting up to discharge our cargo, the forklifts were being lowered onto the back deck and the longshoremen began trickling on board. I had just opened the side door and was preparing to drag the 12 by 12 timber into place. There happened to be one of the longshoremen standing near the side door so I asked him for hand to drag the timber into place. He was immediately in my face telling me in no uncertain terms it was not my job or his for that matter to move this timber. I still don't know whose job it was, maybe they had some more men standing around doing nothing who were designated timber movers. All I wanted to do was get started on the discharge and this was not going to happen without that timber in place, so I grabbed the timber and pulled it the few feet need to block the door. Well, you would think I had committed a capital crime, which in the eyes of these highly unionized labourers I guess I was guilty as charged. He started screaming at me and poking me in the chest with his finger. Screaming about me taking away his job, I had no right to do what I did, he was going to have the discharge stopped, the ship would be black listed, and on and on. He finally ran out of steam and the discharge got under way, despite his threats. After his rant I guess he must have felt he had run a marathon and needed a nap. He made a bed from some dunnage up against the steel wall of the ship's side and promptly went to sleep with his head resting on this steel wall. On the outside running the length of the enclosed cargo area was a catwalk on both the port and starboard sides. We had various tools at our disposal inside the cargo hold, things like brooms, shovels, pry bars, and a large sledge hammer. So I carefully paced out the position of this guy from the side door. So many paces from the aft edge of the door and how high his head was resting against the side wall. Then picking up the sledge hammer and starting from the door I paced out his position along the cat walk on the outside of the ship. Noting about where his head should be on the inside, I swung the sledge hammer as hard as I could aiming for where I had calculated he was sleeping. I left the sledge on the catwalk and whistling a merry tune casually sauntered back to the side door and slipped inside. To say he was a little disoriented would be putting in mildly. He kept shaking his head back and forth trying, I guess, to clear the ringing in his ears.

CHAPTER 3

MV HENRY CHRISTOFFERSEN

IN BETWEEN MY TRIPS ON THE Howay and the Tanu I worked for a summer on the MacKenzie River aboard the pusher tug Henry Christoffersen sailing a thousand miles of river between Hay River and Tukteuktat. As far as my seafaring jobs go this was the bottom of my list. To say I hated it would be putting it mildly. What was there to like, there was no navigation to speak of, as second officer I was nothing more than than a higher paid deckhand, the insects, flesh eating black flies and fighter jet sized mosquitoes, were everywhere, 24 hour daylight which messed your day/night rhythm, and on top of that we had the worst cook in Northern Transportation's fleet. Speaking of which, after only about trip number two upon arrival back in Hay River the captain, a huge bear of a man, grabbed the cook by the scruff of his neck and literally threw him off the boat. I think it was the chief mate who tried to stop the captain sighting union rules or something. It didn't matter, the cook was gone never to return. That night the chief mate and I went through the fridge and freezer and threw overboard all sorts of unidentifiable molding putrid looking stuff masquerading as food.

After returning to Hay River after each trip we adjourned to the only bar in town, the Back Eddie. It was also the only place to get something decent to eat. The chief mate and I became friends and would usually head there for a burger and a beer or two. We never stayed for more than two beers each, partly because the price of booze was astronomically high. That didn't stop the rest of our crew or the crews off the other boats. Because our season when the river was ice free was very short, June through to September, we were payed a years salary for only a few months work. I have it on good authority that more than one person who worked that summer spent their entire salary in that bar.

    Pushing barges down river was a challenge. It was like driving a car on a sheet of ice. In a car on a dry road in order to turn a corner you turn the steering wheel which turns the cars fronts wheel and around the corner you go. If you did the same maneuver on ice, the cars front wheels may turn but the car keeps going straight ahead. The tug would tie 3 massive fuel barges in line ahead, then attach smaller barges 2 and 3 abreast on each side of this line up. The three centre line barges were connected to the tug and each other with steel wire rope tensioned with manual powered winches. The barges on either side were secured to the centre line barges with three inch diameter double braid nylon ropes, very strong. The river was up to a mile wide at some points but only a narrow portion of that was navigable, the rest being shallow with hidden sand bars and boulders. These tugs drew only a foot or two of water. The propellors, four of them were in tunnels to reduce draft. Also to reduce draft the rudders extended only about foot into the water. In order to have enough surface area for the rudders to be effective there were eight of them, four on either side of the centre line. The hydraulic ram that drove these rudders was attached to the four on one side only. The other four were connected by a pipe tie bar to the driven four. When you approach a bend in the river going down stream with the current you have to take into account this car/ice situation and start your turn literally miles ahead of where the bend is. We were approaching a curve in the river with a full tow of barges when all hell broke loose. The link bar between the driven and non driven rudders broke which caused the non driven four rudders to lock hard over one way, while the hydraulic ram drive four rudders were hard over the other way in anticipation of the up coming bend in the river. As far as making the turn nothing happened, we kept moving straight ahead right into the bank of the river, which at that point was ten or twenty feet high. We were travelling at maybe 18 knots, a combination of the tugs speed and the speed of the current. I watched in horror as the lead outboard barge on one side tried to climb the river bank. I actually thought it was going to turn over end for end. Then all the rest of the outboard barges on both sides started to break their mooring lines. It sounded like cannon fire. When the nylon lines snapped they produced a cloud of confetti like snow. We lost every single barge except for the three centre line ones. It took us two days to chase down all the barges and re-assemble them into a tow.

CHAPTER 4

FISHERIES PATROL VESSELS

FPC Howay

I only worked on the Howay for one trip as second mate, so there is not a lot to write about. The Howay and her sister ship the Laurier were two ex RCMP boats dating from the 1940's. They may have been old but they had a certain charm about them. The only memorable experience happened while tied up in Victoria. The chief mate, another shipmate who loved adult beverages, came to me just before heading ashore for the evening, and asked me to hold onto his wallet and not give it back to him under any circumstances until the following morning. OK, an unusual request I thought at the time, but I was happy to help him out. Happy, that is, until he was back on board around two AM and drunk as I ever seen anyone and pounding on my cabin door demanding his wallet back. He was really out of control, yelling and screaming, swearing like only a sailor can, and pounding on my door so hard I thought he was going to break it down. I did contemplate handing over his wallet but was too frightened to open the door. Fortunately, other crew members were awakened by the disturbance and came to my rescue. Lesson learned, don't do any favours for a drunk.

FPC Tanu

The Tanu was a beautiful ship, purpose built in 1968 in Victoria. We were approaching Winter Harbour, on the North West coast of Vancouver Island, one day in some pretty nasty weather when we got a call about a fishing boat in distress off Brooks Peninsula. Brooks peninsula just out into the Pacific Ocean about a two hour sail south of Winter Harbour. There were storm warnings for the West coast of the Island at that time. We did an about face and headed back out to search for this boat. The only problem was that they did not know exactly where they were. We were in communication with them trying to find out where they actually were. We finally found them, but they were only a few miles off the entrance to Winter Harbour and no where near Brooks Peninsula. One of their stabilizer poles had broken in the rough seas and the boat was listing a bit to the opposite side. We tried to get a line over to them but in the rough seas and the Tanu being a fair size ship we were attempting the impossible. The captain would circle around time after time trying to pass as close to the fishing boat as possible while we tried desperately to get a heaving line across to them. The only person we saw was a woman on the bow attempting to catch the heaving line. After multiple passes she did manage to catch it once, but with the very rough sea conditions and the howling winds she lost it. Their boat was still under power and it did not seem like they were sinking, so we suggested they follow us into Winter Harbour. When we got them into calmer water I, along with a seaman or two were sent over in the rubber boat to help raise the remaining stabilizer pole and secure their rigging in order to get them into the harbour and tied up alongside the government dock. When I first stepped on board I found only two people on board, the woman we had seen braving the elements on the bow, and a man lying prone and groaning on the wheelhouse floor. As soon as the woman stepped into the wheelhouse she started savagely kicking him. I can still hear her words today, "get up asshole we have company". I don't think it was more than a few minutes after getting the boat secured to the government dock, when the woman appeared suitcase in hand. The last I saw of her was walking down the dock with one arm in the air giving the one finger salute.

Some of the crew of the Tanu loved to play practical jokes on any unsuspecting sole to cross their paths. A lot of their jokes were crude and not very funny. However, one stands out. At that time there were foreign fishing boats, stern trawlers, that were allowed to fish in Canadian waters off the west coast of Vancouver Island. To keep them honest, the department of fisheries would put a fisheries inspector on board these ships to record their catches. I am guessing they must have had a quota system in place. These inspectors worked month on, mounth off. We would take a new inspector out to the trawler for his month on and pick up the inspector who was scheduled for his month off. I don't know where Fisheries found these guys but they were not among the brightest light bulbs in the box. I don't think they were paid all that much, but they did give them a shiny new uniform complete with a Sam Browny belt adorned with a counter, a hole punch, and a few other accessories. We had just retrieved one such inspector after his month aboard a very rusty and dirty Russian trawler. The first thing he does is head for the shower. After scrubbing himself squeaky clean he liberally applies some under arm deodorant and dons his shiny clean uniform complete with the aforementioned Sam Browny belt. What he didn't know was that someone had pried the ball from the top of his "Ban" roll-on deodorant, emptied out the contents, and replaced it with the juice from a can of sardines. Several people in the wheelhouse were in on the prank, so when he appeared on the bridge resplendent in his shiny new uniform they started sniffy the air for the foul fish like odour. One of the prankster was walking around the bridge sniffing the air when he zeroed in on the hapless inspector, finally getting close enough to him to try and sniff his arm pit. Then the jokes started, "I guess when you spend a month on a dirty rusty fishy Russian trawler the smell must get in your pores". The poor inspector then lifted his arm to smell his pit area and agreed with the comments. He then heads back to the shower, applying more of his adulterated Ban deodorant, and another clean shirt. When he got back to the bridge everyone was laughing so hard he knew something was amiss and he was the target.

Another duty for us was looking out for American tuna fisherman, who would come into our waters chasing the tuna. If we caught them, we were to impound their boats and send them down the coast to Vancouver where they faced some sort of legal action. On one afternoon we caught three of these tuna boats. After they were boarded and advised by the fisheries officer that they were in violation they were told to immediately head for Vancouver where their vessel would be seized. To make sure they complied with this order we would place one of our own on their boat. The fisheries inspector would go with one boat, someone else on boat number two and me, as low man on the totem pole, on the third boat. My particular charge was crewed by a family, husband, wife, and a couple of their children. This family was very religious, not sure of what denomination. After every sentence they spoke, they would end it with the phrase, "praise the lord", and I mean everything. Would you like a cup tea dear, "praise the lord". The weather is very nice today, "praise the lord". I have to go to the head, "praise the lord". They completely ignored me, acting as if I were not there. They offered me nothing, not even a glass of water or cup of coffee, not that I expected them to. At some point the Tanu sent over a boxed lunch for me. Fortunately, I only had to go as far as Port Hardy, the

Tanu needed her second officer back, where I was replaced by someone from the coast guard. Good luck buddy, better pack a lunch.

Sometime before I joined the Tanu, the crews of both the Howay and the Laurier, as well as the crews of the Tanu, were asked to recommend a design for a new fisheries patrol vessel. The Howay and the Laurier were soon to be retired. Apparently, every single person asked was of the opinion that the Tanu was the ideal sort of vessel and therefore just build a copy. Well, the powers that be ignored this advise and instead commissioned a completely new and untested design, the FPV James Sinclair. She was built out of aluminum in Vancouver and proved to be utterly unsuited to the seas off the west coast of Vancouver island. I never served aboard her but friends who had told me they feared for their lives if caught in any sort of blow with winds over about 10 knots. Because she rolled so violently from side to side cracks would routinely appear in her superstructure. As a result, after every patrol she had to pay a visit to the ship yard for repairs. I think she only lasted about 10 years and was retired. The Howay and the Laurier were still going strong after over 40 years. The Tanu is still in service today.

CHAPTER 5

EDWARD O VETTER

AFTER LEAVING THE TANU I GOT a job with Geophysical Services Incorporated on the MV Edward O Vetter, a seismic ship. She was originally built as an offshore supply vessel, the Brenton Shore, on the east coast, registered in Pictou Nova Scotia. GSI bought her and converted her to seismic work. GSI, by the way, was formed back in the late 1930's. At that time there was no one who manufactured the necessary electronic equipment needed for recording seismic data, so the principles formed a company to manufacture the electronics called Texas Instruments. You may have heard of them. Edward O. Vetter was one of the founders along with Cecil H. Green. You may also have heard of him as well. We worked mostly in the Arctic Ocean in the summer months when the waters were ice free. In the winter months we headed south and worked off the coast of Oregon and California. This was a two month on, one month off crew rotation, which for me turned out to be more like nine weeks on and three weeks off. We also worked a 12 hour day which meant for every two days worked I would log three days of sea time. At first I was not that happy with this two and one cycle, not enough time at home which always seemed to pass more quickly than the time spent on board, but after a time I did come to appreciate at least one aspect of this arrangement. I would accumulate sea time a whole lot quicker than the average sea going job, three hundred and sixty five 8 hour days in nine months of actual time spent at sea as apposed to say working for BC Ferries where in would take 5 or 6 years to accumulate that coveted sea time.

    I first joined the Edward O in Nome Alaska. I was flown first to Anchorage then in a small bush plane to Nome. Nome has no alongside berthing. Ships visiting Nome anchor off the town and use their own boats to commute back and forth. In my case I was picked up by the ships lifeboat and taken out to the ship. The lifeboat pulled up to the stern of the Edward O and as I was scrambling up the sloping ramps used to deploy the guns, two or three guys jumped into the boat and headed ashore. The first thing to do when joining a new ship is to report to the captain with your discharge book. That's when I found out that one of the people who departed for shore in the lifeboat was actually the captain. So now what? I was the brand new chief officer and one of only two deck officers on board, the other being the captain. When a ship is manned, whether she is at anchor or under way, there has to be someone on watch on the bridge. At least that is what I was taught. For the next two days I ate and slept on the bridge wondering what I had got myself into this time. Finally the captain, chief engineer, and couple others returned to the ship a lot worse for wear than when they had left it. Through extremely blood shot eyes and stinking of whiskey fumes so bad that if I had been smoking a cigarette I risked a major fire standing too close to him, he told me to get the anchor up and head for the Arctic Ocean. Talk about a trial by fire, at this point the furthest I had ever sailed was the west coast of Vancouver Island. He then retreated to his cabin and locked the door. So off we went. I plotted a course through the Bering Strait and up into the Chukchi Sea, but after that I had no idea where we were supposed to go. Fortunately by that then the captain had had enough time to sober up and sleep off two days of gambling and drinking untold amounts of booze. Welcome to the Edward O Better and my sea going home for the next two years.

I mentioned earlier, the gun trays, which I had used to gain access to the ship from the lifeboat. The guns were actually a large stainless steal piston device that used around three thousand pounds of air pressure to produce the shock wave needed in the seismic process. There was a gun tray on each side of the ship, the aft end of which came very close to the water. There were maybe ten or fifteen guns in each array. They were lowered into the water by sliding them aft from these gun trays and supported on the surface by many large orange inflated balls called scotsmen. These guns when fired produced a shock wave that travelled down to the sea floor, reflected back to the surface, and picked up by the hydrophones in the seismic cable. The cable was wound onto a large drum situated between the gun trays. It was two miles long and contained, every few feet, hydrophones used to record the shock wave from the guns. In the case of a seismic ship there are two crews, the ship's crew and the seismic crew. Around 30 people in total.

The next month, from the middle of September until early November 1982, we spent working at the top of the world in the Chukchi Sea and the Beaufort Sea. The summer was rapidly coming to a close though, the weather was cold and overcast, with days of freezing rain. Time to head south before the ship was iced in. In fact we almost didn't make it out. Point Barrow, the most northerly point in North America, is a choke point between the Chukchi Sea and the Beaufort Sea where the sea ice first accumulates. The seas can be ice free either side of Point Barrow but blocked entirely at this choke point. When we finally decided to leave it was almost too late. Approaching Point Barrow we encountered thick ice and were immediately brought to a stand still. We were stuck. We could not move forward nor could we move back. Some of the crew actually got off the ship and went for a walk on the ice. We were in the midst of making plans to leave the ship right where it was for the winter and evacuate the crews by helicopter when along came our knight in shining armour in the form of a NOAA, (National Oceanic and Atmospheric Administration), icebreaker. It turned out we weren't the only vessel caught in the ice that year. There was another NOAA ship iced in not far from our location who had called their buddies to come to the rescue and they had agreed to free us as well. So we made it out by the skin of our teeth. Next stop San Fransisco.

That winter, late November 1982 until April 1983 we spent working off the coast of California in an area around Point Conception and into the Santa Barbara Channel between the Channel Islands and the coast. Point Conception was an extremely difficult place for us and for the other four seismic ships working the same field. This was the entry point for cargo ships heading for or leaving the port of Los Angeles. On top of the half dozen drilling platforms littering this area and the cargo ships coming and going, you had all the oil supply boats servicing these rigs as well as yachts and all manner of other water craft. Now imagine towing a two mile long fragile seismic cable or streamer, through this armada without getting run over by a passing ship or fowling it on the oil rigs, all the while staying clear of the other seismic ships and their steamers. However, another less than stellar captain managed to do just that, by wrapping the streamer around a drilling rig. In the two years I served aboard the Edward O I don't think I had the same captain twice in a row. Well, our captain managed it, no problem. He came too close to one of the oil drilling platforms and snagged the streamer on one of their mooring chains, all the while boasting to the party chief, "watch how close I can come to that rig." The cable was pulled off the aft end of the Edward O and the whole two mile long thing was taken by the current and wrapped around the rig. The ship board end was on the bottom somewhere but the tail end was supported by the tail buoy which was now under the oil rig. I tried without success to get the ship into a position where we could snag the tail buoy and haul it away from the rig. It was too risky. I risked damage to the ship and the platform both. The next plan was to send yours truly in the lifeboat get in under the rig, lasso the tail buoy and drag it out to where we could get a line from it to the ship. Mission accomplished. However that was not the end of the story. These seismic streamers are really just a big, about six inch diameter, clear plastic tubing through which runs all the wiring for the hydrophones, compass sections, depth indicators, and birds. The hydrophones record the shock wave, the compass sections let the technicians know if the cable is in a nice straight line, the depth indicators allow them to know if each section of the cable is at the correct depth, and the birds, wing like devices, give them the ability to adjust the depth of each section. So, lots of very thin little wires and electronics. To keep water out of the cable, which would run amok with these wires and electronic components the cable is filled with a special fluid, called isopar. But if a break in the plastic tube should occur and water gets inside, then everything shorts out and the cable or that section becomes useless. Each section is ninety meters long. After the current wrapped the cable around the oil rig many of these sections were holed. Pulling it off from around the rig did further damage to the point where the entire two miles of cable was essentially garbage. Don't quote me on this but I would guess a brand new streamer would cost in the neighbourhood of one million dollars in 1983.

After retrieving our badly damaged streamer we were ordered to Port Hueneme where a new cable would be waiting for us. Arriving and securing alongside it was all hands on deck to man handle the old cable off the ship and man handle the new one onto the drum. This took quite a few hours of heavy manual labour and we were all very thirsty. We were allowed ashore but given a time to return as the pilot was booked and they wanted us back to work ASAP. There were only two bars in Port Hueneme and we only had an hour or so to quench our thirst. Myself and the chief engineer went to one quiet bar had a beer and headed back to the ship, while the rest of the crew went to the other bigger louder bar and didn't return. We had a company agent who would organize what ever we needed while in port, in this case, the new streamer. When I got back to the ship I went to the bridge to get my end of things ready for departure, while the chief engineer went to the engine room to do his thing. I waited, along with the pilot, for the crew to return, but no crew. Our agent finally hopped in his van and set off to retrieve the errant crew. He went to the first bar, found some of the crew, loaded them in his van and drove back to the ship, dropping them on the dock, and headed to the second bar for the remainder of the crew. Meanwhile, back at the dock, the first group, as soon as the agent had left, hotfooted it back to the first bar. When the agent arrived back with the second group, surprise surprise, the first group were no where to be seen. Dropping off group number two, he headed off to try and coral the first group. This time, though, when he arrived back with group number one he brought with him a large quantity of beer, which he unloaded on the dock along with group number one. He then proceeded to head out again after group number two. I am watching all these shenanigans from the bridge along with the pilot who was shaking his head the whole time. When the agent had herded the crew on board, some of whom had to be carried, we were finally ready to get underway. The captain finally appeared on the bridge, although not in the best of shape. The pilot had us cast off and had not even given any manoeuvring orders when the captain hollers,"full speed ahead" and promptly keels over backwards and passes out. The next thing I know is the pilot has scurried from the bridge, down over the side, into the waiting pilot boat and was gone. The ship was only a few feet from the dock, and I was the only person on the bridge, other than the body snoring away on the deck under my feet, in a harbour I had only seen for the first time a few hours before, and it was after midnight and very dark. Somehow I managed to get us out of the harbour and into the channel, heading north back to the Point Conception field where we were working. A little late but we made it. Someone, a member of the seismic crew who was not as inebriated as the rest of the gang, supplied me with sandwiches and coffee all night until we arrived back at Point Conception the next morning.

This sort of thing might sound comical in the telling, but believe me it is anything but. Two years earlier another of GSI's ships, the Arctic Explorer, departed Newfoundland for their assigned work area off the coast of Labrador. Many of the seismic crew had been making the rounds of the local bars and were, so I was told, extremely inebriated. Sometime that evening the ship started taking on water and developed a list which grew worse in a short period of time, and finally resulted in the ship sinking. Most of the crew managed to make it to the lifeboats with the exception of thirteen who went down with the ship. The story I got, and this is hearsay, were that some of these crew members were so drunk and passed out they could not be roused to save their own lives. I know all this sounds like I was working with a bunch of drunken no good for nothing types, but in reality they were a very hardworking group. They worked in the most trying of conditions on land in the tundra, the deserts, and the jungles of the world living in tents and trailers. At sea they worked in freezing conditions in the Arctic to the sweltering tropics for months on end.

Just south of Point Conception is the city of Santa Barbara. We spent several months working this part of the Santa Barbara Channel, which separates the northern Channel Islands from the coast of California. Our lines ran in an east west direction. This meant that when we finished a line travelling in an easterly direction we came within spitting distance of the city of Santa Barbara, so close in fact we could see people walking the streets with the naked eye and they, of course, could see us. We were able to tune into the local radio stations and listen to the news, talk shows, and music, and after a bit we started hearing people phone in to complain about this big ugly seismic just offshore. In the very early days of seismic exploration they used a charge of dynamite to create the necessary shock wave, but that went out with the dinosaurs. Our air gun arrays however, did produce a loud explosive sound and an upheaval of water when they were set off. If you have ever seen a WW 2 war ship dropping depth charges on a submerged submarine, that is exactly what it looked and sounded like and these guns would go off roughly every fifteen seconds. At first these calls to the radio station complained about us dynamiting the channel and killing all the fish. I guess someone must have clued in to the fact we were not dynamiting the waters but creating the shock wave with a powerful blast of compressed air. The focus then shifted to the migrating whales who use the Santa Barbara Channel, heading south for the winter. The calls really started to heat up then, with people phoning in from far and wide. It seems someone came up with idea that our shock waves were forcing the whales to abort their young, gotta love those California tree huggers. This went on for awhile when some government agency decided to put an observer on board to monitor this whale situation, or lack of it. I have never in all my years of working aboard seismic ships even remotely witnessed any damage done to the local marine life. No dead fish, no whales aborting their young, nothing. In fact we have had seals hop up onto the gun trays, while the guns are going off, to escape killer whales. On another occasion we had a whale rubbing itself on the side of the ship to remove barnacles, all the while the guns are doing their thing, and that was in Santa Barbara channel. Recent research, however has shown that seismic shock waves do indeed affect marine wild life, but we didn't know that in the early 80's. So one day we were sent a very eager young marine biologist come to document our destruction of the local sea creatures. When he stepped on board he was weighted down with cameras, binoculars, light meters, and Lord knows what else hanging from straps around his neck. He was so encumbered he had to be helped up to the bridge, where he took up the whole chart table with his gear. We had set up a cabin for him, but right from the start he refused to leave the bridge, asking that his meals be sent up for him. This kid was eager to say the least and he was going to save those whales no matter what. For the next couple of days he stayed glued to his binoculars, scanning the horizon for signs of whales, of which there were none. After several days of no sleep and no whales, someone convinced him to go to his cabin and get some sleep. We would call him if we sighted any whales. One of the crew was posted outside his cabin and as soon as he judged him to be asleep, he started pounding on the cabin door, "whales whales off the port bow". There were no whales, of course. When he arrived on the bridge half asleep and out of breath, everyone was most apologetic, "you just missed them, they were right here alongside, you should have been here". We kept this shared up for another day when he finally admitted defeat and left the ship. He never did see any whales, or seals for that matter, nor even one dead fish.

After completing the Point Conception and Santa Barbara surveys in mid April 1983 we were ordered to San Fransisco for repairs and restocking in anticipation of another winter in the Arctic. We were also gifted with a brand new captain. I don't know from under which rock they dragged this him, but I do know he was incompetent, ignorant, and a little bit off his rocker to put it mildly. He joined the ship in San Fransisco shortly before we set sail for the Arctic, first stop Dutch Harbour. This guy had a really bad nervous tick in one eye. Whenever he was unsure of himself or if he was the list bit upset over some trivial matter, his eye would start to twitch, and the more upset or unsure he was the worst the tick became. At times it was hard to watch him. I learned very early on that the worst the tick became the more unstable he would became. We were tied up in San Fransisco for a couple of weeks loading stores, making repairs, and generally getting ready for the summer season in the Arctic. The day we departed the whole Bay area was enveloped in a thick fog. The pilot got us out of the bay, under the Golden Gate Bridge, and headed in the north bound traffic lane. When it came time for the pilot to leave the ship he handed the reins over to the captain and pointed out, on the radar screen, the various blips representing ships either inbound or outbound in our immediate vicinity. The radar at that time was not too far different from what you would expect of a WW2 era unit, very primitive by todays standards. The small, only eight inch diameter screen showed a return for any ship or buoy within range, but that was it. If you wanted to know a vessels heading or speed you had to plot him on the reflection plotter with a grease pencil. This could take 15 or 20 minutes placing a grease pencil mark on the plotter every 6 minutes for the target in question. Then you draw a line through these dots to find out if he is on a collision course or not, which still doesn't tell you his course or speed, and if you have say 6 or 7 targets the officer of the watch is a busy little beaver to say the least. Archaic to be sure, especially when you consider modern radars with touch screens and computerized plotting. When the pilot was pointing out the various targets to the captain, I could see his tick becoming more pronounced by the second until it was taking over the entire side of his face, I knew or expected what was to come. It is customary for the junior officer, me, to escort the pilot to the boarding ladder and safely off the ship, but not in this case. The captain, face twitching a mile a minute informs me he will escort the pilot to the boarding ladder, but will return momentarily. He never did come back. I didn't know where he had gone or when he would return. He finally showed up hours later when the fog had cleared and we were safely out at sea. Next stop Unimak Pass and Dutch Harbour, several thousand mile away. Unimak Pass leading through the Aleutian Island into the Bering Sea would be the first land we would site since leaving our berth in San Fransisco. At that time our only means of navigation was LORAN C, which was fairly reliable. However, Captain Tick, having not seen any land for a couple of weeks and typical for the Aleutians the weather was overcast and raining with visibility only a mile or two, was convinced we would not site the pass as intended and instead bump straight into an island. Consequently his tick had become progressively worse in the days and hours leading up to our entry into Unimak Pass. I might add that I was solely responsible for the navigation since leaving San Fransisco. If he even knew how to use the loran I never found out. We made it safely and tied up at the fuel dock in Dutch Harbour. That evening was the party.

The seismic industry, as is the entire oil business, a dry operation, no booze anywhere on board ships, oil platforms, or shore side installations. So I don't know if that was the reason or not, but management, and this happened all over the world, loved to throw lavish parties for all the people involved. These affairs were usually held in a hotel ball room like setting and included food, sometimes sit down dinners, and all the liquor one could consume. I've attended many of these affairs, some very tame, and others literally ending in drunken brawls. One such party took place in a hotel in Dutch Harbour Alaska only hours after our arrival. A bunch of company big shots had flown in for the affair. Each of these men in turn would stand up and tell us what a great job we were doing and let us know how much we were appreciated, blah blah blah and on and on. This was a sit down dinner situation, with drinks before hand, of course. Unfortunately I was seated next to the captain. When the waitress came around to take our drinks order, I ordered a glass of wine. She said that because there was about 40 people in the room and she was the only waitress that she would bring me a bottle of wine instead. No problem. The problem came when Captain Tick heard this and thought that was a pretty good idea, so he ordered a magnum of some cheap fizzy champagne like substance, Baby Duck. When waitress came back with our drinks she carefully poured a smattering of wine in my glass, leaving the bottle. She tried to repeat the process with the captain's brew, carefully removing the cork and attempting to slowly pour a small amount into his glass. He would have none of that, he grabbed the wine from her hand and raised it to his mouth taking a huge swallow directly from the bottle, none of this pussy half ounce in a dainty wine glass for him. Of course, you can imagine the results of this violent manoeuvre. It started to fizz up with him spraying wine from his mouth over half the table, at which time he slammed the bottle back on the table, which immediately exploded in a volcano like fountain of purple fizzy wine. He made matters worse by trying to stopper the eruption by placing a finger into the open neck of the bottle and in the process again sprayed the table with the ejaculate. While this was going on the company suits were taking turns making their "ra ra" speeches about what a fine bunch of lads we were and how we were holding up a long standing company tradition of one of the finest seismic crews in history. I was more interested in avoiding the splash over from an increasingly plastered Captain Tick and thinking about crawling under the table, when I noticed his tick starting up and getting worse as the speeches went on and he became more inebriated. I didn't know what to expect but decided to make myself scarce, so I took the opportunity to go to the washroom where I tried to hide out as long as possible. After relieving myself, washing my hands, checking my front teeth for an errant piece of spinach, and re-combing my hair several times, I was joined by the chief engineer who had the same desire as myself, and that was to put as much distance as we could between us and Mr. Tick. After what seemed like a long time we decided to head back to the dining room and rejoin the festivities. When we rounded a corner leading to the dining room we found Mr. Tick on his feet, waving his magnum of Baby Duck, and shouting obscenities at the company suits. I still don't know what his beef was all about, but what ever his complaints were he was making sure the whole room could hear him, all the while peppering his drunken speech which expletives that would make even the raunchiest of seamen blush. Just as I was about to turn and run for the hills, a couple of people grabbed him and forcibly frog marched him from the room. I never saw him again, praise the Lord. The chief and I were then able to return to the party and a lovely dinner. No mention was ever made of the idiot, it was like he never existed. You will note I stopped referring to him as captain and instead started using the title of Mr., even though he didn't deserve either honorific.

On a foot note, later that evening I was asked to head back to the ship and move it to a different berth. We had originally tied up to the fuel dock, but there were new customers waiting in line for fuel. The company reps were never going to allow Mr. Tick anywhere near their ship ever again. I think if I had the right certificate in hand I would have received a battle field promotion to captain then and there. Sadly, I was still sailing with a First Mates home trade certificate.

That summer and into the fall, we worked all over the Arctic region, from the Bering Sea to the Beaufort Sea. The Beaufort Sea survey came first while the area was still ice free. Later we moved south into the Bering Sea which remains mostly ice free all year. This doesn't mean it is a calm tranquil body of water however. If you have ever watched that TV show about the Bering Sea king crab fishermen, you will get some idea what it was like. Crew changes during this time took place in several locations such as Wainwright, Barrow, and Dutch Harbour. There are few harbours in the Beaufort Sea part of the Arctic Ocean so crew changes were made by helicopter.

One such crew change took place at Barter Island, a DEW line sight, on September 1, 1983. Back in Vancouver the weather was still warm and sunny, but in the Arctic winter was already making its presence known. The temperature was close to freezing with blowing snow. I think there was about ten or twelve of us scheduled to fly home that day. After you have been on board for two months the outgoing crew members are extremely keen to be on their way, with everyone trying to be the first in line when the helicopter arrived, most of them wearing summer clothing. The helicopter that came for us was quite small and only held about four passengers. On top of the passengers we also sent off the seismic data we had recorded for the previous month. This data was recorded on large real to real magnetic tapes and were packed in boxes about two feet on a side, which meant 3 passengers plus boxes of seismic data per trip. When it departed with the first three scantly clad eager beavers, no one knew how long it would take to get to Barter Island and back. It turned out to be at least a one hour round trip. Also what we didn't know was what we could expect when we arrived on Barter Island. You would think maybe a small warm building of some kind. Wrong! There was nothing, absolutely nothing, not even a blade of grass, let alone a tree in sight, except a cold wet wind sweeping across a gravel runway. No warm building, not even the aircraft that would fly us to Anchorage. I don't know what held me or the chief engineer back but we elected to remain on board in a nice warm wheelhouse sipping cups of hot coffee and watch the other crew members jostle for position to be first in line, when the helicopter returned for the next lucky individuals. When our turn came it was trip number four, the final one. Arriving on Barter Island the twin Otter aircraft that was to take us south was just landing. I literally walked from the helicopter to the aircraft, a distance of about ten feet in a manner of seconds. The first 3 groups who had left the ship hours before, especially the first group were frozen half to death, dressed as they were in short sleeve shirts and in at least one case, shorts. Their only saving grace was the weather on the island was a few degrees warmer than out at sea and the snow had switched to freezing rain.

After another cold wet summer in the Arctic we were ordered to proceed to Hong Kong. Our departure port was from Dutch Harbour where we took on a full load of fuel, groceries, and spare parts. Before departure we had to have some emergency welding done on the bow plating. We had cracked the plating sometime that summer bunting heads with some fairly thick ice flows. The Edward O had an ice strengthened hull. She was not an ice breaker, but the hull plating, especially in the forward sections, was at least one inch thick. She also sported two ducted propellers called Kort Nozzles which were supposed to increase the efficiency of the propeller, more on that later. So before leaving Dutch Harbour we had some patches welded over these cracks in the bow plating on the outside. We were scheduled for a haul out upon reaching Hong Kong so these patches were a temporary fix until we reached Hong Kong. Off we went, transiting through Unimak Pass and turning our nose westward and the South China Sea and eventually Hong Kong. For the next couple of weeks we pounded into at least fifty knot head winds day after day. We tried tacking left and right of our base course to ease the constant pounding on ship and crew, to no avail. Because of these brutal head winds and seas, our speed was greatly reduced, sometimes only managing six or eight knots as apposed to our usual twelve knots. I don't recall how long the trip actually took, but it seemed like forever.

    Arriving in Hong Kong Harbour we picked up our pilot who took us to anchor to await customs and immigration. When the immigration folks arrived on board we all had to line up with our passports for inspection. Unbeknownst to me or anyone else on board our captain, who was from Vietnam, did not have a passport. All he had was something akin to landed immigrant documents from Canada. We were then informed that because the Captain was a stateless person, we were all considered stateless, and would not be allowed ashore under any circumstances. Just what we wanted hear, after several weeks of pounding our way across the North Pacific. What we wanted to hear, of course was, the shore boat would arrive shortly and we could get off this bucking bronco of a ship and finally stand on dry land without having to maintain a death grip on anything that was within reach, and relax with a beer or three. It was not to be, but fortunately, and I was amazed at how quickly the situation was resolved, we only had to wait about 24 hours. At least we all got a good nights sleep after two weeks of being bounced around like those ping pong balls in a wire cage you see on TV when they are choosing the next lucky millionaire lottery winner. It seems our Vietnamese captain had been an officer in the Vietnamese navy during that little war that we all remember so well. After the fall of Saigon he was sent to a prisoner of war camp from which he eventually escaped making his way on a leaky old boat along with 90 other refugees to Japan. While in japan he came to the attention of the then Premier of Nova Scotia who ultimately sponsored him for a move to Canada. I don't know who our captained phoned that night in Hong Kong, but he was issued a passport 24 hours later.

After we were finally cleared to enter the country the ship was moved to a dry dock and hauled out of the water. When the dock was pumped out and we could get a look at the bottom, the first thing I wanted to check out were the Kort nozzles and the propellers. When we were beating our way through the ice, chunks of ice would break off and be sucked in by the propellers and through the nozzles. When this happened the noise was deafening and the whole aft end of the ship would buck and jump around. Naturally we thought the propellers would be damaged in some way, if not, then the nozzles. However both the propellers and the nozzles were in perfect condition, except for the fact that all the paint in that area was gone and the steel was so polished it looked like stainless steel. The aft end of the ship had survived so it was now time to check out the bow. To our horror the entire section of the bow forward of the collision bulkhead was gone. The stem bar was still there, but the one inch thick plating was folded back from the stem and up against the collision bulkhead. You could almost drive a small car through the gap. This area, accessed through a hatch on the deck above, had been a bosun's store were we kept ropes, paint, and spare this and that. I had been in this compartment before leaving Dutch Harbour while they were welding the patches on the outside, and everything was fine. During the crossing to Hong Kong the weather was so bad, the bow deck was almost constantly under water and there had been no way to get to this store room even if we wanted. The theory was that water had filled this compartment and with the ship repeatedly plunging up and down in the seas, a panting situation had led to the cracks spreading and finally splitting apart. Like folding a strip of metal back and forth until it breaks. After shaking our heads and an inspection by the classification society, the Chinese dockyard workers were called in to make repairs. I watched in amazement as half a dozen workers began taking measurements with a length of knotted string, no tape measures to be seen, and recoding their readings in a tiny notebook with only a two inch long pencil, all the while chattering away in Chinese. A week or so later they were back with a whole new wedge shaped bow section complete with the shelving for the store room. We waited with bated breath as the crane lowered the section in to place, it fit perfectly.

After our refit we worked in the south China sea for a few months. About the only memorable thing I can recall about this time period was that the food we were served was so bad know one knew exactly what we were eating, still don't. On a plus note some enterprising member of the crew discovered that the price of a plane ticket to repatriate us to North America when bought in the USA was at least, if not more, than twice the same ticket if bought in Hong Kong. What transpired was that we were issued a ticket by the company for a one way trip from Hong Kong to Vancouver at a cost of around $700.00. We would then go to a travel agent in Kowloon and cash in that ticket and then immediately buy the same thing back for say $300.00. To this day I don't know who figured out this little scam, or how. Leave it to a seaman.

After our Chinese adventure we were back to the Arctic and the coast of California. I didn't bring the ship back to the Arctic but did join it again in Point Barrow, Alaska. At the same time there was a new chief engineer joining for the first time. We had to spend a couple of days together in Barrow at the Top of the World hotel. Point Barrow is a dry community which didn't bother me, but the new chief engineer was constantly complaining about this, why, why, and on and on. At first he seemed like a decent sort but after two days of his bitching about the lack of liquid refreshment I was starting to re-evaluate my opinion of him. He, at some point, found out you could buy a bottle of bootleg whiskey for around $100.00, and wanted me to go in for half. That would probably be closer to $300.00 in todays money. I will admit that I was all for a beer or two but $50.00, or $150.00 today, for a half bottle of cheap Johnny Walker Red whiskey was way over the top, so I said no. From there his demeanour towards me went south. I was never so glad when the helicopter arrived to take us out to the ship and I could be rid if this jerk. When we stepped off the helicopter to be greeted by fiends and ship mates it was like coming home. The new chief engineer, however, said nothing to anyone except show me the engine room. After a quick, maybe 15 minute tour he retreated to his cabin with the words, "get me off of this ship." I don't know where GSI found these idiots, mostly captains, and now a chief engineer, but if I was in charge of personnel I am sure I could have done a much better job. After that one brief visit to the engine room he refused to set foot in it again and refused to even set foot outside his cabin. To get him off the ship it was decided to drop him off at a DEW line site somewhere on the north slope of Alaska. We arrived offshore of this site and I was detailed to put him into the lifeboat and take him ashore. Our regular chief engineer, and an old friend was there to meet us. It was a very calm day, cold, but at least calm. Off I went with a couple of seamen and the idiot. It was so calm that I decided to nose the bow of the boat up to the beach, have him jump off, grab the new chief and then back off. Every time we came close to shore the seismic crew took the opportunity to send any data we had collect off as well. So along with dumping off the idiot we had to unload several boxes of tape. So far so good, then disaster struck, a small wave, small enough I wasn't concerned about it, slapped the stern of the lifeboat and pushed it broadside to the beach. We all immediately jumped over board in freezing water to try and keep the boat from lying broadside to the beach. No good, no matter how hard we pushed and shoved, standing in water up to our waists, we could not get the boat off the beach. Now what? We were stranded? We did manage to get a fire going and warm up and dry off, sort of. I was in contact with the ship so I wasn't alone in trying to devise a plan to get us off the beach. There was even talk of flying in some sort of rescue team. Eventually, the ship cobbled together every bit and piece of rope they could find, attach a gun float to one end and drift the this menagerie of ropes into the shore where we were able to grab it and were eventually pulled off the beach. It turned out there was a considerable current flowing in towards the beach which we were unaware of at the time. Although this current is what got us stuck in the first place, it was also our saviour, allowing the buoy and attached ropes to drift in to where we could grab ahold of it.

When I was next due for time off, I was met by our agent in Anchorage. GSI always paid for our air fare and expenses travelling back and forth. The agent hands over our tickets and usually buys us a farewell drink before we board the plane. It was over this drink that I asked what became of the idiot chief engineer. I was told he was flown to Anchorage by helicopter and then told to find his own way home. Apparently, the place where the helicopter landed and the Anchorage airport are not that close to each other. The agent even tried to get him to cough up money for the ticket they had bought him to get to Alaska in the first place. I don't think he got very far with that request but I could be wrong.

During my two years with the Edward O Better I did get to see some interesting places. One such place was Herschel Island in the Beaufort Sea. We had anchored in Pauline Cove for a partial crew change, not me unfortunately, to land supplies and to offload the seismic data. A twin Otter aircraft with huge balloon tires landed right on the beach. I was tasked with running the rubber boat back and forth between ship and shore, taking off going crew and seismic data into the beach and incoming crew and supplies out to the ship. We were there most of the day so I was able to explore some of the island. What I remember the most was walking through the grave yard and inspecting all the grave sights and markers. The island was used by the whaling fleet in the late 1880's. Because the season was so short the fleet would spend the winter in the bay, so there were many crosses with the names and dates of people who did not make it home, John Smith died 1884, for example. Tuktoyaktuk was another place I was able to visit on several occasions. As with all the Arctic regions it is a desolate and uninviting place, for me anyway. It is way above the tree line, just the odd patch of hardy grass, lots of sand and rocks, and not much else. The saying was that Tuk is not the end of the world but you can see it from here. I did manage to buy a T-shirt that read in big letters, TUK-U and in small letters the university of the north. Some other places include Wainwright Alaska, McKinley Bay NWT, Inuvik NWT, Fairbanks Alaska, Homer Alaska, as well as the already mention, Nome and Anchorage Alaska. While working in the Bering Sea I was able to get ashore on Saint Lawrence Island, how I managed that, I have no idea.

Another island in the Bering Sea, Saint Mathews Island is very close to the border with Russia. The lines we were shooting at that time were drawn right up to the border, which is just a line on a chart. However, because the streamer was two miles long, we had to steam two miles into Russian waters before turning and heading back to Alaskan waters. Remember we are talking 1983, the cold war may have been winding down but not quite yet. Every time we crossed that invisible line into Russian waters, a couple of military jets would appear to keep an eye on us. They would stay with us until we crossed back over the line and then disappear. I don't know where they came from or where they went, but every time we got close to the border, there they were. Some of these planes flew very close to us as they did their fly by. I rememberer one aircraft was so low that standing on the bridge I was actually looking down on it.

What I thought was to be my last trip with the Edward O, ended at Point Barrow Alaska on September 9, 1984. I had completed my ON 1 certificate earlier in the year, which was as far as I could go working in home trade waters and collecting home trade sea time. Home Trade is described as all the waters of North America extending offshore for 200 miles. The ON 1 certificate qualified me to serve in the capacity of master home trade or chief officer foreign going. Now it was time to make the final leap to Master Mariner, but first I need to collect one year of foreign going sea time. So after arriving home and only staying for a very short month, I booked a ticket to Hong Kong.

After a year away from home and sailing half way around the world I was back home and working on my

Master Mariners certificate, when I received an unexpected call from GSI. They asked me to fly to Alaska and sail the Edward O Vetter from Dutch Harbour Unalaska, to Seattle Washington, where she was to undergo an extensive refit. I would be sailing as her master, my first appointment as captain. The trip south from Alaska was uneventful. After arriving in Seattle, I thought my obligation was over and was looking forward to getting home and back to my studies. The company agent, whom I had known for some time, tried to convince me to stay on. However, when I declined he came up with a plan. I was to work on the ship Monday, Tuesday, and Wednesday. They would then fly me to Vancouver so that I could attend school on Thursday and Friday. Friday afternoon they would fly me back to Nanaimo so that I could spend the weekend with Louise. Monday morning they would then fly me back to Seattle for my three day work week. All of the flights were at their expense, plus I was on full salary the entire time. I suppose they thought I would make a good captain for them after all the losers I had sailed with the last two years. I spent the next two and a half months overseeing the refit, all the while shuffling back and forth between Seattle, Vancouver, and Nanaimo. In that time I had duly completed my Master Mariners Certificate of Competency. I was now a fully licensed Foreign Going Master and could serve as captain of any ship of any size any where in the world. That is when, for what ever reason, the price of oil fell from $25.00 a barrel to around $12.00 a barrel and the seismic industry went into a tail spin. Ships were laid up and their crews laid off, along with yours truly.

CHAPTER 6

MV FORTUNE KING/MV SLEEPING BEAUTY

MV Fortune King

Even while I was working for GSI I had been applying world wide for a job on a foreign going ship in order to write for my next ticket, Master Mariner, without success. I don't recall how I came up with the idea, but the plan was to fly myself to Hong Kong and knock on doors. Somehow I had discovered this free book published by the Hang Seng Bank of Hong Kong. This book had a section which listed all of the shipping companies in HK, all I had to do was get to Hong Kong and waltz into the banks head office and ask for a copy. Book in hand I would then pound the pavement knocking on doors begging for a job. Well it didn't quite work out as planned. First though, I had an introduction from a chap who ran a restaurant in Nanaimo and was from Hong Kong. His sister was a major player in one of the worlds largest shipping companies based in Hong Kong. He wrote me a letter of introduction, which was all in Mandarin, so I have no idea what he had said in this letter. Upon arrival in Hong Kong I checked into the Seaman's Mission in Kowloon. This was a wonderful place, restaurant, bar, bowling alley, olympic size swimming pool, and very cheap rooms, around $10.00 per night if you were a seaman. My first stop the next day was to get my hands on the Hang Seng shipping guide book. Before this I had also joined the Hong Kong Merchant Navy Officer's Guild. The next thing I did was to look up the offices of my friends sister's company. It was big, I think they had their own building. Letter in hand I presented it and myself at the main reception desk. I was told to wait for a minute or two after which a nicely dressed gentleman appeared and asked me to follow him. I was escorted into a sumptuous board room panelled in teak with orential carpets and plush upholstered furniture and offered a cup of tea in fine bone china cups. I think my thoughts at the time were that this was going to be easier than expected. Enter, Nancy, my friends sister. She was every inch the high powered executive type from her clothing to her hair and makeup and then some. She sat down across the table from me, neatly placed a legal pad and pen in front of her and asked me what she could do for me. I said I was looking for a job on one of her ships. Her whole demeanour changed in the blink of an eye. She told me to follow her, showing me a door that led to a set of concrete stairs, almost pushed me inside and slammed the door. Up until this point I had only seen lushly appointed offices and hallways bustling with sharply dressed executives and their assistants. Now I was faced with a dank, unpainted concrete, dimly lit stairwell, leading down to who knows where, but with no other option I descended. Thinking about it later I can only assume Nancy thought I was there to charter one of her ships or something along those lines. When I had first entered the building I had used a wood and polished brass elevator to get to the 10th floor reception. I was now walking down, not quite in the same style as I had ridden up. When I got down I found myself in grimy smoked filled room used by crews looking for their next billet. So much for my Nanaimo friend's recommendation.

Let pounding the pavement begin. I started with the big names in shipping in the high rise district of Hong Kong. After a week or so of disappointment I was forced into the low rent district and the one room one man offices. The pay for a ship's officer in those days was so low as to be almost non existent. I was looking at only a few hundred dollars per month for a nine month contract. However, it wasn't the money I was interested in, it was the sea time. Many of the shipping offices I visited were sceptical of my reasons for applying for a job on a ship with Chinese officers and third world country crews. I think I came close at least twice in my search, but they felt a token white boy among an all oriental crew would not be in their best interest. At least I got to see many interesting places in Honk Kong. One of my stops, if I happened to be in that part of town, was the Royal Hong Kong Yacht Club. Because I belonged to the Nanaimo Yacht Club, I was able to, as a visiting yacht club member, gain access to their club house and most importantly the bar. Here I could, after a long day of walking all over Hong Kong Island, relax with a cold one and rub shoulders with the rich and powerful.

Finally, one day, success. I managed to land a second mates job with a one ship, one man company, aboard the MV Fortune King. I was in, or so I thought. The good ship Fortune King was a standard design massed produced inexpensive ship, built to replace the aging fleet of WW2 Liberty ships. This design was known as an SD14. The name stands for shelter deck, 14,000 DWT, (deadweight tons.) Over 200 of these vessels were built in yards around the world starting in the late 60's and continuing through the 70's. SD14s had four hatches forward of the accommodation block and one hatch aft and was fitted with union purchase derricks for cargo handling. The Fortune King must have been one of the first built, given her sorry state of neglect.

My Journey

In order to join the ship, I was flown from Hong Kong to Dhaka in Bangladesh. In Dhaka I met up with several other members of the crew, all officers and all from mainland China. I got some Holy S*#t batman stares from them, as if to say, "who is the whitey"? We were put on a very rickety old school bus for the drive to Chittagong on the coast. That trip was an adventure in itself. The bus had no padded seats, only bits of plywood where the seat cushions should have been. The bus had a split windshield but with only glass on the drivers side. Before I noticed this omission I grabbed a seat right up front on the right side, the better to enjoy the view. The view I got was OK when the bus was stopped, but underway I was assaulted with the exhaust fumes from the buses and trucks in front of us belching black oily diesel fumes along with the dust and dirt kicked up by their passage. That part of Bangladesh is flat and low lying and barely above sea level. There was water every where, flooded fields, ponds and rivers, several of which we had to cross on small ferries just as rickety and dilapidated as our bus. My heart was in my mouth more than once when these ferries would, belching huge clouds of black diesel exhaust, pull away from one bank of a river and struggle manfully towards the opposite shore. In every case these ferries were crammed to the gunwales with mostly trucks and buses, leaving only a few inches of freeboard. The other wonderful aspect of that road trip was the road itself. It was a two lane road barely wide enough to allow a truck or bus to pass each other safely without loosing at least one side mirror. Come to think of it I don't think our bus had a side mirror on the drivers side. This road was also heavily crowned in the middle, the better to shed the torrential rain showers common there. This meant that if the bus stayed in his lane it would adopt a very large starboard list, and the same for vehicles travelling in the opposite direction on the other side of the road. Consequently, every vehicle, whether they were coming or going travelled in the middle of road thus avoiding this starboard list. The fun part was when it came time to move back into your lane and avoid the oncoming vehicle. The drivers of these buses and trucks would literally wait until the last moment both swerving mightily into their own lane and then back up to the centre line in one very well coordinated manoeuvre. When we arrived in Chittagong we were put up in the Hotel Hawaii for a couple of days to await the arrival of the crew who were for the most part from Sri Lanka. While staying at the hotel which by western standards would be called the Hovel Hawaii, we hung out on an open air balcony overlooking the street below. As this is a Muslim country there is no alcohol to be seen, unless you know where to look, more on that later. So for liquid refreshment we were limited to Coca Cola in the old fashion glass bottles. There was always, on the street below, a group of street children dressed in rags and begging for anything we could give them. My Chineses compatriots ignored them completely as if they did not exist. I, however had a soft spot for them. After finishing my Coke I decided to throw the empty bottle down to these street kids. It was caught by a young girl who was a little taller than everyone else in her gang. She grabbed it and tried to run away. I was horrified when a hotel worker chased after and beat her mercilessly to get the bottle back. Talk about culture shock. I did meet her again in the months I spent in Chittagong and managed to slip her and her band of beggars a few coins, probably not more than a few pennies in western currency.

While on the topic of these street urchins, the ship I was assigned to was not going anywhere in a hurry, also more on that later. I quickly found out that in Chittagong there was only a couple of places one could get a beer. One was the Hotel Agrabad, a huge step up from the Hotel Hawaii, and the other was the Hong Kong Cafe. So after standing my watch I would head ashore for a beer at one of these fine establishments. I first tried the hotel because it was a short distance away from the Hotel Hawaii, which I had spotted while staying there. It was a very posh place place with armed guards allowing only the most well healed patrons entry to the premises, I guess I must have fit the bill. About a block away from the hotel I was surrounded by the band of street urchins which included, the coke bottle girl. I had been warned, before leaving the ship, not to carry anything valuable in my pockets, don't even wear a wrist watch, or you will loose it. When I approached the hotel for the first time I was surrounded by this mob of twenty plus kids begging for a hand out. I had purposely filled my pockets with coins of the local currency which was almost worthless for a westerner. When the kids first ganged up on me, maybe they recognized me, I had them calm down and handed everyone a coin or two. The sheer delight on their faces and their excited chatter was enough to warm the heart of Scrooge himself. As I approached the hotel they were hanging on to every part of me for dear life. By the way, I never lost anything that I did not give them voluntarily. The problem arose when the guard at the hotel gate spotted me and my band of urchins. I called him Lurch, he was huge at least seven feet tall. He came charging out into the street with a baseball bat and started to beet the kids, thinking I was being attacked or something. On future visits to the hotel, I still gave the kids coins, but I had them stop around the corner from the hotel so I could approach the entrance alone. I have a picture of these kids.

Sometime later I discovered the Hong Kong Cafe which served beer. It was a bit of a walk, especially up and over the bridge spanning the Karnaphuli River, so one day I decided to enlist the services of a pedal cab. It was powered by a little guy who must have weighed close to 100 pounds soaking wet. The bridge was elevated so that ships could pass underneath. This meant an uphill climb from ground level to the peak and then a downhill run to the opposite bank. I had watched other pedal cab drivers struggling up this steep incline toting two over weight gents reclining in the back of the cab. The incline was so steep it would have been a struggle for the cab by itself, let alone the extra baggage of a passenger or two. When my cabby got to the bridge I would hop off and help him push the cab up the incline, then hop on for the ride back down. I don't recall exactly how much I paid my driver for his services, somewhere in the neighbourhood of fifty cents for the round trip to the Hong Kong Cafe. After a few days of this I guess he felt he had a steady customer or maybe I was paying too much, so he started sleeping on the river bank next to the ship. When ever I appeared he would leap up and dust off the cab and escort me to my seat. One day I had a craving for a nip or two of scotch whiskey. There are no such things as liquor stores in Chittagong which meant buying it on the black market. I asked my cabby if he may be able to help me out in this regard. I didn't have a whole lot of money, but I did have a few American dollars which I was reluctant to change into the Bangladesh Taca in case I needed it in the future. I also had some American cigarettes which I had bought on the ship and which turned out to be worth as much as the local currency. I think I paid around two dollars for a carton of Winstons. I didn't smoke myself but I would pass them out to the longshoreman working the ship. You would think I was giving them $100.00 bills. I had a twenty dollar bill which I showed my cabby and asked him if he could get me a bottle of whiskey. Off we go into the back streets of Chittagong where I am positive no white man had ever set foot before or was even crazy enough to do so. My cabby took me down a winding narrow dirt road lined with stalls selling everything from brassieres to ball bearings. He dropped me off at a stall selling band aids and pencils, took my $20 and peddled away into the sunset. My first thought was that I had just lost my $20. My next thought was, how am

I ever going to find my way out of this maze of stalls and back to the ship. I had no choice but to let events unfold as they may, so I hauled out my trusty packet of Winston cigarettes and started passing them out to the shop keeper and his buddies, who up until that moment had been giving me the evil eye, big time. I am sure I saw one them caressing his knife. As soon as the cigs appeared their demeanour change dramatically. They were smiling, laughing, and patting me on the back. I did breath a sigh of relieve but still wondered how long I should wait for my cabby to return before I took off on foot or until the cigs ran out. Thankfully he did return with a bottle of Johnny Walker Red label scotch whiskey, and get this, he gave me change from my twenty in American dollars. Just before arriving back at the ship he took the bottle back and hid it somewhere on his person so that police guarding the gate that gave entry to the area where we were tied up would not confiscate it.

Before I get too carried away with life in Chittagong I should probably fill you in on the good ship, MV Fortune King. To say this ship, and I use that word loosely, was a rust bucket would be doing it a favour. I have never seen, let alone stepped foot on a ship which was one step away from the scrap heap. There is a ship breaking yard in Chittagong, which was where this pile of scrap metal belonged. To make matters worse, I was sold a bill of goods by the company in Hong Kong. Remember the whole point of this exercise was to accumulate sea time and experience for my goal of becoming a master mariner. The company man I met in Hong Kong had shown me a picture of a ship which I assumed was the Fortune King, wrong, it was a colour glossy picture of a brand new cargo ship just leaving the builders yard on its maiden voyage. On top of that he had told me that the ship was trading world wide, wrong again. The actuality of it was that it was little more than a barge. The entrance to the Chittagong harbour is fairly shallow, allowing only smaller shallow draft vessels to come alongside for discharge. The larger deeper draft vessels would anchor in the roads and ships like the Fortune King would steam out, secure alongside, and be loaded with what ever cargo was destined to be offloaded in Chittagong. I don't even think the ship was capable of steaming anywhere as the main engine was a pile of parts on the engine room deck. The one time we had to move the ship we were towed to a fuel berth to top up the diesel tanks. The diesel was needed to run the generator which ran the winches and house keeping services. So much for my valuable sea time. Apart from that one move, we were tied to the river bank my entire stay.

    The accommodation aboard the ship was not only filthy dirty, but everything you would associate with living quarters was either broken or non existent. Except for the captains cabin there was one washroom shared by all the officers. The toilet was full to the brim with poop and toilet paper, the biffy was a wooden outhouse affair hanging over the stern. There was no running water for a shower. I had several buckets in my cabin and a tap under the sink. The third mate kindly showed me the routine, place bucket under tap and wait for a day or two for it fill, take bucket into washroom and pour contents over head. The mess room was a bit better but no five star rating. There was one long table where all the officers sat to eat. There were no condiments anywhere to be seen, ketchup, or salt and pepper like you would see on any other ship in the world. We were fed a bowl of rice three times a day. In the morning the rice would be topped with a fried egg, for lunch it would be topped with a piece of seaweed or something green, and for dinner the rice was topped with a prawn or a questionable piece of fish. The curious thing about the meal times was that no one would start eating until we were all seated. If I was a few minutes late I would arrive to find the whole gang sitting there like they were frozen in place, but as soon as I took my seat it was chop sticks flying and don't get in my way. The times when our rice was topped with a prawn were the worst show of table etiquette I have ever witnessed. The table top was covered in a clear plastic sheet. These prawns were of the jumbo variety. The only thing was they were served whole, gut, legs, feelers, the whole meal deal. My compatriots would pop the whole pawn in their mouths, body, shell, guts, and start chewing. Then with a delicate manoeuvring of the chop sticks pull the unwanted portions of said crustacean from their mouths depositing the bits and pieces on the plastic table covering next to their bowl of rice. Apart from these sit down meals there was nothing to eat or drink, no coffee, no tea, no snacks nothing. I learned later that some of the crew, while I was off a my quest in search of beer, were spending their time ashore in search of food.

All ships the world over must undergo a safety inspection every year, things like fire fighting equipment, life boats, and rafts, that sort of thing. Our inspection happened to coincide with my tour of duty. I had sometime earlier given the lifeboats a cursory inspection and determined that there was no way they could be launched sort of using a couple sticks of dynamite. They might as well have been welded in place. So when the inspector showed up I was hoping to point out a few of these glaring problems to him. Didn't happen, he was ushered into the captain's cabin, the door closed, and after a couple of hours, the door opened and he left the ship. Inspection complete. The captain or maybe the chief officer had typed up some bogus inspection certificates, giving the current date, which were to be pasted to the fire extinguishers. The only problem was that there were no bottoms in these extinguishers, they had rusted completely away. You could stick your arm in the bottom and reach all the way to the top. One day I wanted to charge the fire mains in order to hose down the decks. It was pointed out to me that the mains, a three inch diameter steel pipe was also rusted out, you could put your fingers up into the pipes at many locations. So no lifeboats, no fire extinguishers, and no fire mains and hoses.

As second officer I was in charge of navigation. One of the first things I did first was to check out the bridge for the necessary charts and publications and make sure they were up to date and to see what sort of equipment was on board for navigation, or lack of. I didn't find a whole lot and what I did find was so out of date they might as well have come over on the Mayflower. I made a list of the things I would need, it was quit extensive, and presented it to the captain. When my order arrived it contained one pencil.

When I first joined the ship we were unloading a cargo of sugar in fifty pound sacks. The longshoremen would descend into the hold where the derricks had placed several pallets, one for each man. They would then each load their pallet with bags of sugar, maybe thirty bags per pallet. When a worker finished loading his pallet, the operator manning the union purchase derrick would lift the load from the hold and deposit it on a barge we were moored to. The ships were tied up along the banks of the river, no docks or piers. To keep the ships away from the river bank there was a barge placed amidships between the ship and the bank. The derrick would drop a loaded pallet onto the barge. From the barge up to the top of the river bank was long wooden plank. Each longshoreman, when his loaded pallet had reached the barge, would scramble up out of the hold and down onto the barge, grab each bag of sugar in turn and run up this gang plank and deposit his bag onto the back of a waiting truck. After he unloaded his pallet he would return to the hold and repeat, and when I say they ran, they did just that. I think they were paid by the bag, so the more bags you moved in a day the more you were paid. I am probably exaggerating, but I think they earned less than one dollar a day for this exhausting back breaking work.

As second officer my watch was from noon to 4 PM and midnight to 4 AM. While discharging I would stand a cargo watch from noon to four. The discharge only took place during the daylight hours, so my work day was only four hours long. The night watch I spent sleeping or reading, occasionally wandering around the deck but not much else. Which of course gave me ample time to explore Chittagong and drop into the Hong Kong Cafe for an afternoon beer. My duties during my noon to four PM watch were equally boring and non existent. If it had been a real ocean going ship I could have spent time catching up on chart corrections, but with no charts to speak of I had little do but chat up the longshoremen and pass out my Winston cigarettes. The boss of the longshoremen seemed to like being seen with this important white man and was never far away from me, especially when I had cigarettes to hand out. The workers had a sort of coffee shop/lunch room on shore. It seemed like every time I gave him a cigarette he would invite me up to this coffee shop for cup of coffee. I'm sure part of this was to be seen rubbing shoulders with the whitey. When we took our seats on cement benches the proprietor would hustle over with a couple of unwashed cups and very filthy rag, polish the cups and pour us our coffee. Actually once you got past the unwashed cups and the oily black rag, the coffee was quit good.

Every ship that discharges in Chittagong is assigned a custom's official who is present whenever cargo is offloaded. The official assigned to my ship was an articulate well educated young man, and as I found out later, from a very wealthy important Bangladesh family. We spent many hours together discussing, for the most part, the differences between life in the west verses life in the east. He was constantly marvelling about how in the blue blazes I had ended up on a decrepit Chinese ship in Bangladesh. He was most interested in my life in Canada, and I was equally interested in his life in Chittagong. One day he invited me to his home to meet his family. What an eye opener. Chittagong was not your typical pristine tropical paradise, at least the parts I was exposed to. There was garbage every where, most of the buildings were in disrepair and falling apart at the seams, very few paved roads, electricity and running water a luxury, with many people living under plastic tarps anywhere they could find space. To get to his home I hopped on the back of his motor bike. There were not a lot of private cars in Chittagong. After driving through rutted dirt streets we arrived at a walled estate with a guarded gate. Outside the wall garbage was piled every where, with people lining this wall living in their plastic tarp homes. Inside the wall it was if I had been transported to another almost magical world. The beautiful gardens were alive with lush tropical plants and equally exotic birds of every description. I don't know how much area was enclosed inside the wall, a couple of acres at least. There were many buildings all in good condition, clean and recently painted. My friend gave me a brief tour along a curving paving-stone path snaking through the well tended gardens pointing out the function of the various structures we passed. He showed me the kitchen, the maintenance building, the men's building, the women's building etc. I don't know how many people lived in this extended family compound but the motel like building where the men lived had at least six separate apartments. The wives lived in a different building, as did the children and the grandparents. There was also a building for the staff. After our tour he took me up to a long second floor balcony off which were the doors to the men's apartments.

He introduced me to his brother and showed me one of the apartments. His wife then appeared with some soft drinks and left without saying a word or even looking directly at me. The wives were only allowed to enter the men's building by invitation. Once married the wives were never to leave this compound again, ever. Unless I suppose it was on a stretcher, and even then they probably had a grave yard within the walls. On the way out I was introduced to his mother, who had not set outside the walls for over fifty years. She was constantly chewing on betel nut wrapped in a betel leaf along with some sort of white powder. Her teeth, gums, and lips were permanently stained a reddish brown colour. I guess this was how she had survived her fifty year exile in paradise. Talk about a different world.

My friend the customs man would eventually prove to be a life saver. It didn't take me long to realize that I was going nowhere with the MV Fortune King. The big problem was that I had entered the country on a seaman's visa, which was essentially a one way ticket in but not out. I was expected to leave by ship. Lord knows how that was to happen, given the unseaworthy condition of the ship. I had already looked into flying back to Hong Kong on my own but was met with a brick wall at every turn. Part of the problem was the I had no money. I had just about accepted my fate when, if you can call it that, when my situation took a turn for the worse, or better, depending on which side of the coin you are looking at. I became ill. It was like a very bad case of the flu. I would get so cold that I thought my shivers would lead to broken bones, and then in the next instance I was so hot I was sweating buckets, not to mention the vomiting and diarrhoea. I don't know what caused my condition, polluted drinking water maybe or even malaria, who knows. After a few days of this my friend, the customs agent, stepped into help, big time. There was no such thing as a doctor or any medical assistance to be had, so the only option was to get me out of the country. He drafted several letters to be presented to any officials I came in contact with. I don't know what was written in these documents, but I still have them today. He then took me to a travel agent somewhere in the city and you will never guess what I spotted in their window, a VISA sign, Hallelujah Visa, where I was able to purchase a ticket from Chittagong to Hong Kong, via Dhaka and Bangkok.

The night I left Chittagong he took me to the Chittagong Club for drinks and dinner, although given my condition I didn't feel much like eating or drinking. The Chittagong Club is a private club built in 1878 by the British for the officers and gentlemen of the Empire. Sort of a little slice of England for the elite of British society who were forced to endure life in a land far from home. This club came complete with bars, billiard tables, card rooms, smoking rooms, cottages for overnight stays, a swimming pool, cricket pitches, tennis courts, and acres of manicured grounds, with plenty of servants to cater to your every need. What really got my attention were all these dark skinned, rich and powerful Bangladeshes trying to act like the lord and lady of some manor house in England, playing billiards, smoking huge cigars, and sipping their pink gin cocktails, and of course ordering their own countrymen around like the servants they were. I was offered a single malt scotch whiskey in a heavy crystal tumbler served on a silver plater by a uniformed bowing and scrapping servant. I declined the cigar. I couldn't believe it. I had just left a rat and cockroach invested rusting hulk of a ship with no indoor plumbing and three bowls of rice a day to this palatial country club for the gentlemen members of the highest order, no ladies to be seen. Talk about mind blowing!

The next day I boarded a small twin engine aircraft for the short flight to Dhaka. What I remember the most about that flight was the there were many wrecked and burned out aircraft lining either side of the runway as we took off. Goodbye Chittagong and welcome Dhaka. Dhaka had at least a modern western style airport, which was clean and sported the usual assortment of restaurants and shops. My eyes must have been as big as saucers walking into this wonderful cafe where I had the most delicious breakfast of fried eggs and hash browns, and a cappuccino. I was in heaven and the meal made me feel almost human again. After breakfast I was wondering around in a bit of a daze, wondering if I was dreaming the whole experience when I was approached by two young boys, aged maybe eight or ten, who offered their assistance. I think I was in a bit of reverse culture shock plus maybe the illness was clouding my judgement. I handed one boy my ticket and passport while the other took hold of my suitcase. In todays world this would be nothing short of madness. They took me by the hand and led me to the front of a very long line of passengers waiting to check in. They presented the boarding agent with my ticket, passport, and the letters from my friend in Chittagong. Whatever these letters said I do not know, they were written in, and I am only guessing, Hindi or something like that. It was like Moses parting the Red Sea, in an instant my passport was stamped, I was issued a boarding pass, my luggage checked, and then led to the first class lounge to await my flight. I gave the two boys all my remaining Bangladesh Tacas. What ever the amount was, and it could only have a couple of dollars, their faces lit up like they had just one the lottery.

On a final note, after arriving back in Hong Kong and checking into the Seamen's Mission, I took a head shot picture of myself, a selfie, and mailed the film back to Louise. When I finally made my way home to Nanaimo many months later, one of the first things Louise asked me about was who is that man you took a picture of? She didn't recognize me and I didn't even recognize my own picture.

MV Sleeping Beauty

Shortly before I left Chittagong I was walking along the bank of the river when I met some english speaking white guys. The first white faces I had seen in months. We got to talking and it turned out they were from a cargo ship moored not to far from where my ship was berthed. We then exchanged the usual pleasantries, where are you from, what ship are you with, are you deck or engineering? It was a given I was an officer since all the lower deck crews were from a third world country, the Philippines, China, and in the case of the Sleeping Beauty, Poland. After getting the basics out of the way they invited me back to their ship for a beer. What a treat, the MV Sleeping Beauty was what one would expect of a modern ocean going cargo ship of around 30,000 DWT. She had five hatches forward and was fitted with travelling cranes for loading and discharge. The first thing I noticed was that she was clean and in good repair, but she also sported all the amenities, a bar, very important, well appointed en suite cabins, a dinning room with white linen table cloths, a bridge with charts and wonder of wonders, electronic navigation equipment. Although by todays standards, it was very basic. There was no GPS in those days so offshore navigation was by sextant. Right up my alley. After a few beers I guess I must have let my feelings known concerning my present employment and how desperate I was to leave the Fortune King for something along the lines of the Sleeping Beauty. As it turned out their present third officer was leaving after their next port of call, in Singapore, and if I was up for it they would recommend me to the company, AllSeas International Management, which was based in Kent England. I assume it would be cheaper to fly someone from Hong Kong to Singapore rather than from England to Singapore. All I had to do was get from Chittagong to Hong Kong.

I don't remember how the timing worked out or how long I stayed after arriving back in Hong Kong, but somehow I ended up with a ticket to Singapore. Before leaving Hong Kong though, I had to obtain a Panamanian Certificate of Competency. This is no big deal, you just go to the Panamanian Consulate, show them your Canadian certificate and they issue you a Panamanian ticket of equal rank, in my case chief officer foreign going. But first I would have to go for a physical exam, also not a big deal except for one minor hiccup, their regulations for eye sight were a bit more strict than the Canadian requirements. My eye site is 20/20 in the right eye and 20/200 in the left, not good enough for the Panamanians. I was wearing my glasses when the doctor sat me down in front of the eye chart and told me to remove my glasses, cover one eye and read the eye chart. So I removed my glasses, covered my left eye with my left hand a dutifully read the eye chart down to the bottom line, the one with the smallest letters. OK so far. I was then ordered to cover my other eye and read the chart again. I then used my right hand to cross my face and again cover my left eye and read the chart all the way to the bottom. The doctor never noticed my deception but I almost blew it, because he questioned me, why if my eye site was so good am I wearing glasses. I think I mumbled something like, force of habit. The doctor just shrugged and signed off on the medical, I got my ticket, and was off to Singapore. When I arrived in Singapore someone met me at the airport and drove me to the ship, which at that time was in dry dock.

Arriving on board I was introduced to a few of the crew, some of whom I had already met in Chittagong. The officers, deck and engineering, except the second officer and myself, were all from the UK, a couple from Scotland and the rest from England. The crew and the second officer were from Poland. Apparently, because he was Polish, an officer, and a member of the Communist Party he was assigned the task of acting as a sort of a watch dog over the Polish crew. The second officer's name was Walter, no one knew if he had a ticket or not, as he proved hugely incompetent at even the smallest task. When confronted with one of his many screw ups, all he would say was, "Yah Yah." We called him Yah Yah Walter, more on him later. For the first few days while the ship was out of the water we spent our time working on deck. The weather was very hot and muggy. At noon we would break for lunch and cool off for an hour inside the air conditioned accommodation. Everyone first headed for the bar and a cold beer or ten. Not one to turn down a beer I joined the rest of the officers for what I thought would be one beer and then lunch. Wrong; I had my beer and then set off for the dining room and lunch, but the rest of the officers all stayed in the bar for a liquid lunch. There were only four or five of them but during the lunch break they managed to fill a large green plastic garbage container with the empty beer cans. I don't know how they did it. When I went back outside into the heat and humidity after only one beer all I felt like doing was going to sleep. For the next several days while the ship was in dry dock they would repeat this liquid lunch ritual without once setting foot in the dining room. I don't know how many beers each man drank but it must have been at least twelve, give or take. As it turned out this was a crew of, in my opinion, alcoholics, mostly the engineering staff. The chief engineer, first engineer, chief mate, and radio operator were the worst, with the chief engineer topping the list at number one. For the nine months I spent on board the Sleeping Beauty I don't recall ever seeing him eat any food, except maybe the bar peanuts.

After leaving the dry dock we spent the next week or so at anchor. The harbour boasted a fleet of small passenger ferries in case you wanted to go ashore. They would depart from Clifford Pier stopping at the various anchored ships in turn until they were full and then head back to the pier. There was a very nice open air beer garden on the pier, which was the first stop for an evening on the town. I had one beer there but had other plans, I wanted to see the Raffles Hotel and have a drink in the Long Bar. One or two of my companions thought that was a good idea, so we caught a cab and off we went leaving the rest of the group to hold down the beer garden. Singapore is the exact opposite of Chittagong, like night and day. Chittagong is dirty and dusty, with garbage every where. Even the air is polluted from all the poorly maintained trucks and busses belching oily black diesel exhaust. Contrast that to Singapore which is so clean you can eat off the streets. I think it is a capitol offence to discard a piece of chewing gum into the street.

My first trip aboard the Sleeping beauty was to Indonesia and Burma to load plywood destined for the Persian Gulf. We stopped at three different locations. The first port was some where in Burma where we sailed up a large river for several miles where we went to anchor. The plywood came out to us on barges and we used our own cranes for loading. The longshoremen came aboard and set up camp on the aft deck. They brought every thing with them for an extended stay, fire wood, live chickens, pots and pans, tarps, sleeping mats, you name it. They actually built a cooking fire right on the steel deck for cooking rice. The chickens were slaughtered as needed and added to the pot. While loading cargo part of my job was to record the ship's draft every hour or so. Because we were not alongside and you couldn't see the draft marks from on deck, they were hidden from view by the curvature of the hull, we hung rope ladders over the side at the bow and the stern. The theory was you climb down these ladders, note the draft, and then climb back up. Easier said than done. As you climb up or down, the ladders tend to lie against the hull, not a problem when side of the hull is vertical. The problem comes with the curvature of the hull at the bow and at the stern. As you descend the hull curves inward, so that when you reach the point where the hull is curved inward the most, you are now hanging from the ladder in an almost upside down position using mostly your arms and hands for climbing. It is very difficult and only because I was fairly young at the time, early thirties, was I able to accomplish this feat. It soon became an exhausting chore. The gangway was rigged as there were people coming and going continuously. I then got the bright idea to walk down the gangway jump in the water, swim to the stern, note the draft, swim to the bow, note the draft and swim back to the gangway. The weather was very warm, hot even, and the water equally as warm, so no problem, what could go wrong. One of the longshoreman had noticed my swimming draft collection efforts and very excitingly approached me waving his finger in a no no gesture and speaking heatedly in Indonesian. I didn't have clue what he was going on about, I thought maybe I had broken some rule or regulation. I did stop though. Then that evening after dark he approached me again and wanting to show me something. The campers on the back deck were also fishing from the stern in order to supplement their rice and chicken meals. They had hung a light from the stern and suspended it just above the water in order to attract the fish. Unfortunately it attracted more than just fish. As I peered down into this cone of light I could see hundreds of sea snakes twisting and turning around and over each other in an almost solid undulating mass. I was later to earn that these snakes are extremely venomous, and just one bite was enough to kill a man. I never went swimming again.

Our next stop was Palembang, South Sumatra, also located about thirty miles up a long river. We picked up the pilot at the mouth of the river and sailed up it for the next three hours or so. There was not much to see along the way, just dense jungle foliage descending down to the waters edge. Then as if by magic, we came around a bend in the river and saw a neat and tidy little town that looked like it had been transplanted lock stock and barrel from some where in middle America. There were paved streets with curbs and side walks, a brick church, fast food eateries, KFC being one of them, a neat subdivision of cookie cutter homes, in short every thing you would expect to find in Anytown USA. We went to anchor just off this town. At night you could see the neon signs for the bowling alley, the theatre, and other businesses. If I had been knocked unconscious and woke up in this town I would have sworn on a stack of bibles that I was somewhere in the bible belt of USA.

Upon arriving at anchor I went to lower the gangway for what I thought would be the customs and immigration people, they are usually the first on board but not in this case. The first group up the gangway were the madam and her flock of young girls. I met them at the head of the gangway not too sure what to expect or what I should do. I shouldn't have worried because it turned out to be the accepted practice. I found out later that if you don't allow the madam and her harem on board then the customs and immigration officials will find all sorts of problems with the ship. Anyway, madam politely asked me to escort her and her girls to the captain where I found, to my surprise the entire Polish crew lined up outside the captain's cabin. Most of the crew, when we were at sea, seemed to think that bathing, clean clothes and even brushing their hair was optional and at best left for a later date, if ever. Now here they were, scrubbed clean, shaved, hair combed and wearing there finest stepping out clothes waiting patiently for madam and her entourage. Being fairly new to this offshore sailing thing I didn't know what to think, but it seemed to be nothing out of the ordinary for every other member of the crew, just another routine day at sea. The whole process was very well orchestrated. The captain and the madam were holding court in his office, and as each seaman in turn entered with his girl of choice, a few words were spoken between the madam and the captain who would then make a notation in his allotment ledger. An allotment is how much of your pay you have elected to take each month while on board, the remainder being sent home to your family. In my case I chose an allotment of $100.00 per month with the remainder sent home to Louise. Each month we would appear before the captain to receive our allotment less anything you have charge against it for that month. Most of the these charges were from drinks you had purchased in the bar or goods from the bonded stores. In the case of the madam and her harem you would be charged for how many days you elected to keep your girl which was then deducted from your allotment. If you elected to keep you girl for two days, then the captain would make an entry to this effect in his ledger and then pay the madam on the spot. A very efficient system I might add. When the madam had concluded her business arrangements, I escorted her, and a couple of girls who had not been lucky enough to secure a suitor to the gangway and off the ship. As soon as she had stepped into her waiting boat and pulled away, the customs and immigration officials pulled up and boarded the ship. The ship and her crew were then cleared, in record time, to enter the country. I am assuming that the officials more than likely received some monetary compensation for their hand in this arrangement. While I realized that this system was efficient it also alleviated many problems. Problems that led to a host of issues on another ship and another time.

During our stay in Palembang I was eager to get ashore and explore a bit of the Island and its culture. Unfortunately I chose to team up with the chief engineer and his band of drunks. We had to hire a boat to get ashore and so this, at the time made sense, sort of like sharing a taxi. The boats they used were little more than a very long dugout canoe with a big engine on the back. They were only wide enough for one person abreast but maybe forty feet long, and some what tippy. Arriving ashore the chief engineer and his buddies made tracks for the closest watering hole while I set off to explore. They gave me a time to meet back at the bar so we could catch our pre-arranged boat back to the ship. My exploration was short lived however, as we were a long way from any sort of touristy sites. All I saw were dirty muddy roads lined with tar paper shacks, and because it was getting dark lots and lots of bats flying everywhere. So back to the bar to await the arrival of our boat. It was an excruciating wait as the only beverage served was warm soft drinks and warm vodka, neither to my liking. This hadn't slowed the chief engineer and company down though, I had only been gone a short while but when I arrived back at the bar there were already several empty vodka bottles littering the table. Finally it was time to go. Walking back to the boat it was obvious the chief was a bit wobbly on his feet after knocking back probably more than one bottle of vodka. When we started to board the boat the boatman, noticing the chief's inebriated condition, refused to let him into the boat. This provoked a large and loud cry of rage from the chief. The boatman then called the police, who immediately had us all arrested and thrown into the local gaol. Despite the fact that the chief was a loud and boorish drunk he could be quite comical at times. We were all locked in a cell to await sobering up even though I had not had a drop to drink. From the moment the cops were called, actually they looked more like the army, until we were locked in the cell, the chief had been keeping a loud boisterous condemnation of everything wrong in the world including Indonesia, it's people, their economy, etc, etc. When it became clear to the chief that we may actually have to spend the night in the cell, he beckoned one of our guards over and told him if we have to stay here we should at least have some beer and handed him a bunch of money. I guess our guard thought this was a good idea because he grabbed the money and left. I was thinking the chief had just lost his money, either that or we were going to be charged with bribing an army officer, but much to our amazement he returned in short order with a flat of beer. We were then released from the cell and spent the next few hours lounging around the police station drinking beer. At some point one of our guards took off and came back with some of the greasiest take out food imaginable. It didn't take long for the beer to be consumed, but by then it was too late at night to run out and buy more. Again, the chief engineer came to the rescue. He suggested they take us back to the ship where there was ample booze to be had. Good idea. Our guards, there were about six of them, marched us down to the rivers edge, commandeered a boat, and we set off for the Sleeping Beauty. As soon as my feet hit the gangway I was off like a shot for my cabin. These guards or army guys were dressed in fatigues and were armed to the teeth with rifles, side arms, knifes, and bandoliers of bullets. When I woke the next morning for my watch I walked past the bar where all six guards were fast asleep on the deck. Outside the door to the bar they had neatly stacked all their weapons. The rifles were placed in a pyramid shape with the bandoliers, knives, and pistols draped over them. Apparently the chief had told them it is against company policy to bring weapons into the bar. I vowed that I would never again accompany the chief engineer and his band of drunks on an away mission. My vow was eventually broken, but that is another story for later.

After leaving Palembang we made one more stop somewhere in northern Sumatra, coming to anchor in a large bay, to finish loading our plywood, I can't remember where exactly, but it was a short trip in and out. When we were underway and had dropped the pilot it was a simple bit of navigation to reach the open sea. The only obstacle in our path was a large mountainous island, but there was miles of sea room on either side. While we were at anchor we had a power failure lasting maybe a couple of hours. Then when power was restored everything had seemed to be back to normal. Getting ready for sea the captain or the mate on watch or both must go through a check list of items to make sure you are ready to sail, similar to the captain of an airplane. I wasn't on watch for departure, but Ya Ya Walter was and, of course, the captain so I wasn't party to these pre-departure checks. After the pilot was safely away and we had come up to speed the captain had left the bridge in charge of Walter and joined me by the pool. It was a glorious sunny warm blue sky day. I was a bit nervous having the captain soaking up the rays beside me while Ya Ya was left alone on the bridge so I kept glancing forward either side of the accommodation block to monitor our progress. Surprise surprise we were heading directly towards the island in our path. I pointed out this anomaly to the captain. We both thought to give him a minute to change course and clear this island, but when it became apparent that was not going to happen, we both hotfooted it up to the bridge on the double. Entering the bridge, the captain pointed to the island directly in our path and said something to the effect, "what the f#$k are you doing?" Walter calmly pointed to the chart where he been neatly plotting ranges and bearings along our intended course which clearly showed, on paper at least, that we were in fact not heading for the island, despite what we could see out the window. The reason for this discrepancy was the previously mentioned power outage. This outage also meant the gyro compass shut itself off and because the ship was at anchor and swinging back and forth, when the power was restored the ships head was not the same as when the gyro stopped working, it was maybe thirty degrees out of whack. One of the first things you look at when getting ready for sea is to check the gyro compass. Either the captain or Walter or both should have checked the gyro, especially after a power failure. Notwithstanding this error, you could clearly sea this mountain of an island directly in our path just by looking forward out of the bridge windows. Walter however, stuck to his guns, repeatedly pointing to the chart with his meticulous positions plotted using the radar for his ranges and bearings. These radar bearings are tied to the gyro compass. The ranges were OK but his bearings were about thirty degrees off. To say Walter was as thick as a brick would only be doing him justice, he was actually thicker than the island directly in our path. I think around that time I asked the captain what sort of ticket Walter held. He said he didn't know, all had been given was a single sheet of paper written in Polish with Walter's name on. All the certificates I had been issued, as well as certificates from other countries I had seen were in the form of a passport like document with a hard cardboard cover and the details of ones courses and endorsements on high quality paper between the covers. My opinion of this captain was beginning to falter. He was an OK as a person, but not much of a captain. About all he was good for was handing out our allotment and drinking. He took no interest in the running of the ship, I rarely saw him on the bridge, and he never saw fit to check up on his officers to make sure they were doing their jobs. Even when confronted with Walter's incompetence he would shrug his shoulders and simply walk away.

We were now on our way to the Persian Gulf in order to discharge our plywood at ports in Oman, Salalah and Muscat, UAE, Dubai and Abu Dhabi, and Kuwait City, Kuwait. Our first stop was Salalah in Oman. My only memory of Salalah was walking around the port and marvelling at all the old wooden lateen rigged Dhow's, some quit large, that were used for coastal trading. Our next stop was Muscat where we ran into a bit of a problem when entering the harbour. We had picked up our pilot outside the harbour entrance and proceeded under pilotage to enter the harbour. The pilot will use his local knowledge to safely navigate a ship into and out of harbours or through difficult coastal passages. This, however, does not relieve the captain of his duty as captain. Years later I ordered a pilot off the bridge of my ship because, not only was he drunk, but I felt he was endangering my command. The plan for coming alongside in Muscat was to sail straight into the harbour, stop and then back to starboard for a starboard tie up. I was stationed on the stern to direct the seamen and line handlers and follow the orders of the pilot. We sailed a little bit past our berth and then went astern for the swing, with the aid of tugs, into our berth. The only problem was we were not moving. The pilot went a little too far into the harbour and we had run aground and even though we were in reverse and the propellor was churning mightily away stirring up mud all around the stern we were stuck. I knew we were stuck fast and even an engineer poked his up out of the engine room to see why we were not moving, but up on the bridge the pilot, captain, second officer, and a few other people were completely oblivious to the fact. Finally, they clued in and a larger tug was called to pull us off and get us alongside. The ship came off her mud berth as silently and easily as she had grounded in the first place. No damage done. Naturally the pilot blamed the captain and the company had to cough up money for damages to to the harbour and to several tugs. One was to the tug who pulled us off, even though I would swear she had not been damaged in any way. I think the company also paid for repairs to tugs that were not even at the scene. We remained alongside for maybe a week while the blame shifted back and forth, but eventually to get the ship released, the company had to pay up.

This gave me ample opportunity to explore Muscat, old and new. Muscat and the other Persian Gulf cities were a whole lot different in 1984 versus what you see pictured today. There were no glitzy high rise towers stretching as far as the eye could see. For the most part what I found were nicely paved roads and lots of sand. Old Muscat was centered very close to the port with the buildings dating back to the turn of the century. There were open air markets, camels, and the locals dressed like they had just stepped off the set of Lawrence of Arabia and no women to be seen. One afternoon I was invited into the home of a local merchant for a cup of black thick coffee, he was trying to sell me what he claimed were ancient artifacts and extremely valuable. I'm sure he was producing these artifacts just behind the curtain where we sat sipping our coffee, so I declined his offer. From the old town there was a nicely paved road leading up a hill to what would eventually become new Muscat. When you got to the top of the hill there was a four lane modern highway and, as I recall, not much else. At the junction of the highway and the road up from the harbour was a fairly new hotel which boasted an English style pub. The place exuded wealth. The only cars in the parking lot were new Rolls Royces and the clientele were all expensively dressed and bejewelled. I felt like a poor kid from the wrong side of the tracks, but in a muslim country where booze is as scarce as hen's teeth, I was not going to pass up the opportunity to quench my thirst with a mug of real English ale. As I'm nursing my pint, a very elegantly dressed English gentleman with an upper crust Oxford accent, sat down next to me and struck up conversation. This, of course leads to the inevitable questions, "where are you from, what do you do" sort of thing. After I had finished my story he told me he was from England and that he was a salesman. Now

I am thinking he must be selling 747's or Kentucky Derby winning race horses, maybe even Rolls Royce cars. Wrong on all accounts. It turned out he sold bird seed. As you know, the wealthy sheiks are into falconry in a big way. I didn't know falcons ate bird seed, but maybe they kept canaries and budgies as well. Anyway I did enjoy hobnobbing with the rich and powerful, even if this guy was simply a bird seed salesman.

Our next stop was into the Gulf proper through the Strait of Hormuz, first stop Dubai. Dubai in the early 80's was nothing like it is today. There were no glittering glass high rises buildings stretching off into infinity, nothing but the centuries old white washed brick and mortar structures common with the time. I do remember the souk where you could buy everything from chewing gum to diamond and gold jewelry. I bought a new pair of running shoes. The other treat that Dubai held for me was the seamen's mission. It goes without saying that it sported a very nice bar with imported beer from Europe, remember this is a Muslim country and no alcohol to be seen anywhere, not even on board the ship. However, that surprisingly, was not its major attraction for me. It also boasted an olympic size swimming pool. I spent every spare moment happily swimming laps while the rest of the English officers happily downed pints of English ales. I said that we could not even drink on board the ship. A foreign ship, from whatever country, is considered part of its home country no matter where it is located. The theory is, as soon as you step on board a ship registered in England in a foreign port, you are actually stepping onto English territory. This is not the case in the UAE and definitely not the case in Kuwait. In Dubai the customs folks closed and sealed the bar doors, as well as the bonded stores. In Kuwait they actually searched the bar and our cabins for liquor, and then placed everything they found in the bonded stores room locking and sealing the door. First though, the custom officials gave the captain a shopping list, we want X number of bottles of whiskey, X number bottles of vodka, and so many cases of beer, and then they locked and sealed the door. I actually helped them carry their forbidden ill gotten gains off the ship and into their waiting cars. It goes without saying that if the captain hadn't acquiesced to their demands there would have all sorts of problems with clearing the ship by customs and immigration.

After Dubai we made a very brief stop in Abu Dhabi. All I can remember about Abu Dhabi was sand and more sand and nothing else, not like it is today. The only thing that sticks in my mind was during the few hours we were discharging, was the fact we were not allowed ashore, period! There was even an armed guard posted at the foot of the companionway to enforce this edict. As with every situation involving loading and discharging it was part of my job to record the ship's draft. We had the rope ladders rigged for this chore but, since we were alongside and the gangway was down I thought it would be OK to walk down the gangway, stroll up to the bow, back to the stern, record the drafts and re-ascend the gangway. Wrong on all accounts. The guard at the foot of the gangway, who looked like he was about 16 years old and armed with some sort of assault rifle, had been given a plastic chair to sit in while guarding these evil Englishmen. Unfortunately for me he had fallen asleep in his chair and had not noticed me leave the ship. I had checked the forward draft marks and was on my way aft when he awoke and saw me. I think he was more startled than anything and maybe afraid a superior would see what was happening and take him to task for letting me off the ship. He leaped out of his chair pointing his rifle at me, shouting who knows what in Arabic, and gesturing with his rifle to return to the ship. He kept poking me with the rifle barrel to hurry me along, which I was not going to argue with, but I did for a brief second, consider grabbing the rifle and give him a poke or two. Fortunately, sanity prevailed and I returned to the ship unharmed.

Dubai and Abu Dhabi were the stepping off ports for the rest of the gulf. This was also the time of the Iraq Iran war in the early and mid 1980's when Iraq was lobbing exocet missiles at ships sailing through the gulf, mostly oil tankers. I have a picture somewhere of a huge oil tanker tied up in Dubai with a large hole in the side of her fire blackened accommodation block. As we would now be sailing through a war zone we were entitled to danger pay, a whopping ten dollars extra per day. To sail from Dubai up the entire length of the Persian Gulf to Kuwait City took less than 24 hours, 17 hours rings a bell, as a result we did not get the whole ten dollars. Very generous of the company. Like many shipping companies, Allseas International Management or AIM for short, put their logo on the sides of the ships funnel. In our case the company logo was "AIM" in thirty foot high letters painted either side of the funnel. The joke of the day was the suggestion that we should paint over this logo before leaving Dubai. The agent who informed us we would be getting this danger pay also showed us a picture of our sister ship which had been hit with an exocet missile only the month before. One man, the first engineer, had been killed in that attack and the ship sunk. It was known that these missiles would home in on the largest mass of metal it could sense, usually the accommodation block. For this reason, sailing out into the gulf, we would have both lifeboats swung out and the entire crew, except the captain and chief engineer, making the trip comfortably camped out on the bow next to the anchor windlasses. We took some sandwiches, plenty of beer, sunscreen, and cushions for the voyage while the captain manned the bridge and the chief engineer manned the engine room. A few months later I met a chief officer from another ship who had been sailing into Bandar-Khomeini Iran, with a load of cotton and ammunition when it was hit by an exocet missile. They had also been sailing under the same conditions as we had, that is crew on the bow, captain and chief engineer aft. The missile had hit the ship's side in the way of the cargo holds and started a fire in the bales of cotton which were loaded on top of the ammunition. Cotton doesn't flame up like other materials, it just glows red and smoulders and is very difficult to put out. The captain had radioed the chief officer to grab some men and come aft and put out the fire, to which the officer had replied with an emphatic "NO". I think he may have used a few other colourful words, but the answer still remained the same, "no way Jose". They eventually made it in to port where they had to lower every single bale of cotton into the water one at time in order to put the fire out.

Kuwait City was our final stop to offload the last of the plywood. Other than the very strict rules on alcohol, even in the privacy of our own cabins, I remember Kuwait City as much nicer than Dubai, with clean, paved streets, modern buildings and manicured tropical gardens. At the time they were experiencing a shortage of hotel rooms in the city. The solution was to entomb a retired cruise ship in a backfilled sand berth, the SS Santa Paula, cut a hole in her side to act as a front door and call her the Kuwait Marriott Hotel. The Santa Paula was built in the USA and launched in 1958. She sailed primarily between New York and the Caribbean. In 1971 she was sold to Greek owners and then in 1976 to the Marriott hotel chain, when she became the Kuwait Marriott Hotel. She was a beautiful and elegant vessel, but sadly was bombed and gutted by fire when Iraq invaded Kuwait in 1990, and she was declared a total loss. I did go aboard her in 1985, wandered around her fabulous interior, and enjoyed a cocktail, non alcoholic of course, and a selection of pastries in her, "fit for royalty" dining room.

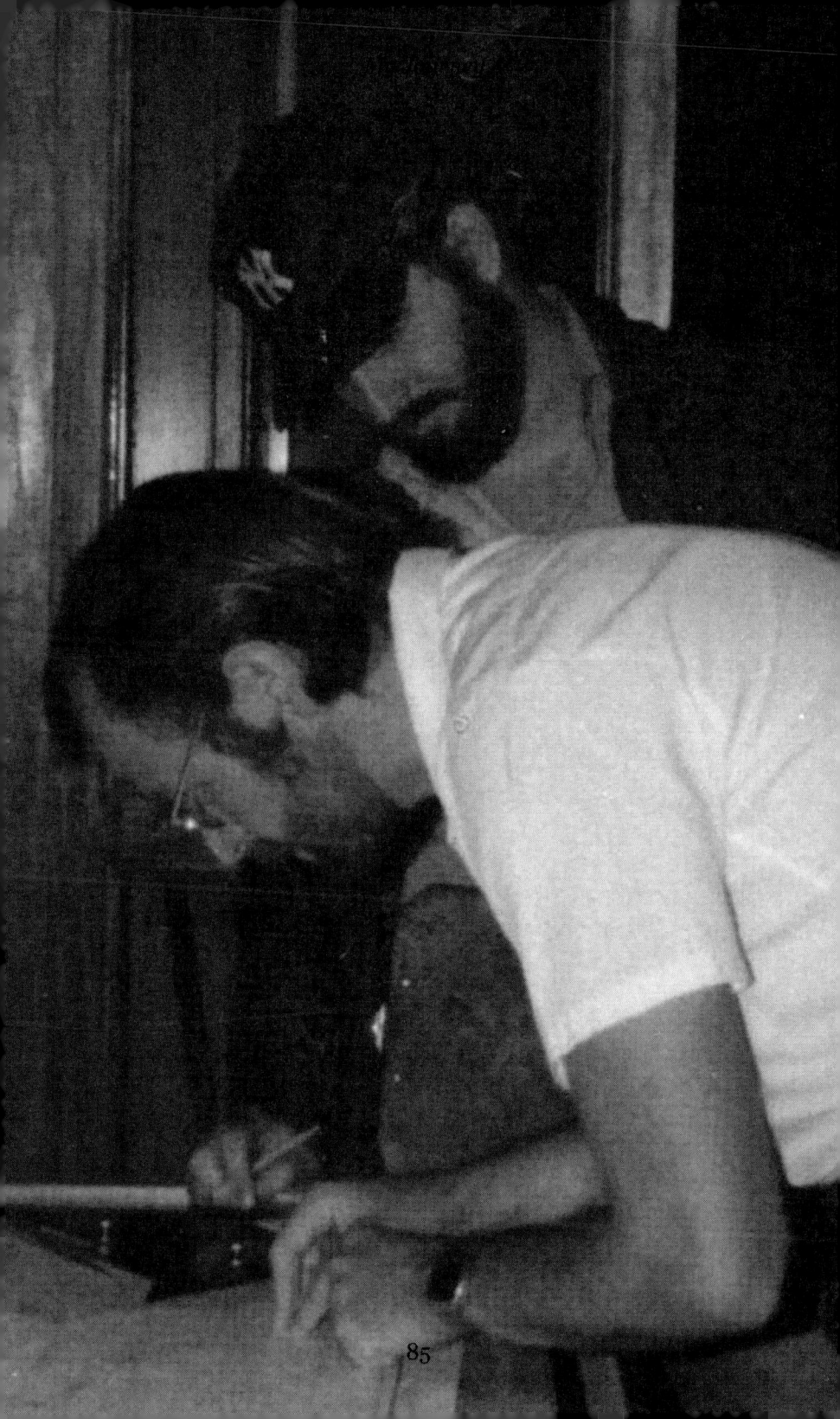

M.V. Henry Christofferson (sister ship)

M.V. Sleeping Beauty

CHAPTER 7
SLEEPING BEAUTY 2

AFTER LEAVING KUWAIT WE SAILED IN ballast (no cargo) to Richards Bay in South Africa to load coal bound for Europe. We were first told we would be taking the coal to England, but along the way the cargo was sold and we ended up sailing for Emden, Germany. After anchoring in Richards Bay we were given some time to pump out the ballast before being moved alongside to load the coal. That is when the problems started, major problems. It is the duty of the deck officers to discharge the ballast and in all respects get the ship ready to load cargo. The Sleeping Beauty had many ballast tanks situated the length of the ship. There were double bottom tanks and wing tanks. These wing tanks extended from the bottom of the hull up the level of the main deck. When we are standing sea watches the three deck officers worked four hours on and eight hours off. When loading or discharging cargo we stood cargo watches. This meant that the second officer and myself, (third officer) actually stood the watches on deck, six hours on and six hours off, which left the chief officer in overall charge and on call 24 hours a day. His responsibilities were firstly, to ensure the ballast is pumped off, dipping and recording the levels in each tank as it is pumped dry, and secondly to ensure the ship was loaded on an even keel in such a way as to minimize stresses on the ships hull. It is not simply a matter of filling one hold with coal and then moving and filling the next hold in line and so on. We had a loading computer which you can use to draw up a loading plan before any coal comes near the ship. The chief officer must then insure this plan is followed to the letter. However my chief officer, being the alcoholic that he was, and the second officer who seemed incapable of writing his own name, these responsibilities were left up to yours truly. With my very limited experience I did manage to draw up a loading plan and present it the captain for approval, OK so far. The first job was getting rid of the ballast water. With the wing tanks you can simply open some valves and let gravity do the rest, up to a certain point. When the water level in these tanks reaches the water level outside the ship you have to start pumping or the water will start re-filling the tanks. After presenting the loading plan to the captain, I started the procedure to discharge the ballast, but by then it was the end of my watch and time to hand the reigns over to Walter for his six hours. I had opened the wing tank valves but had not yet started pumping when Walter took over the watch. I went over the procedure with him again and again to make sure he understood what was to be done and told him to keep dipping the tanks continuously to monitor the water levels in each tank, and went off to my bunk. When I came back on watch six hours later I discovered there was more water in the ballast tanks than when I had left. I could excuse Walter because he was mentally impaired, but where was the chief officer or the captain for that matter?

Richards Bay was a major shipping port for the export of coal. The harbour, however was limited in size for ships either anchoring or alongside berthing. As a result they kept to a rigorous schedule for the arrival, anchoring, and loading of ships. You were expected to arrive on time, go to anchor for X number of hours to discharge ballast, get moved alongside for X number of hours for loading, and leave on schedule.

After our scheduled time for de-ballasting had expired the tugs arrived to move us under the gantries for the loading phase. I guess no one had thought to inform the port that we had not completed our de-ballasting. About half the coal had been loaded when someone clued in and discovered we were already down to our marks. I had just come back on watch to a flurry of activity from, mostly shore side personal running back and forth and sounding the ballast tanks themselves and still no sign of the chief officer. It normally would have taken no more than a few hours to take on a full load of coal, but now our allocated time slot had come and gone and another ship was waiting its turn under the loading gantry. They had to move us back out to anchor in order to sort out this ballast debacle. Still no sign of the chief mate or the captain, and it goes without saying that Walter was not going to be of any help. Our piss tank of a chief engineer came to the rescue, surprise surprise. He and I organized a de-ballasting plan which was made much more difficult now that we were half full of coal. We were forced to pump ballast up and overboard against the weight of tons of coal already onboard. I can't remember the timing, but let's say getting rid of the ballast water from an empty ship would take maybe 12 hours, while a ship full of coal was going to take 24 hours. I stayed up for the entire time, however long it took, it seemed like days thinking back on it now. We then had to wait for another time slot to finish the loading, which gave a couple of us a chance for a run ashore. Remember, I said I would never accompany the chief anywhere after our Palembang excursion, well I thought under the circumstances a minor celebration was in order. The chief engineer and I had never really seen eye to eye. I guess I didn't drink enough to be included in his circle of buddies. The dining room and bar on board were separated by a set of double doors, always left open. So while I was sitting down to my dinner, the chief and his circle were as usual holding forth in the bar. The chief would routinely make snide remarks concerning the Canuck who was not good enough or too high and mighty to join them for cocktails. On this occasion it was once again a cab sharing situation to get from the port into town, so off we went. When we arrived at the hotel bar and had settled in for what I hoped was no more than a drink or two, we gave our order to the bar tender. I ordered a glass of white wine, this being South Africa after all. The chief would have none of that, "bring the lad a bottle of wine". I don't think I had finished even half the bootle when it started to come back up and I had to rush to the men's room where I was violently ill. I don't know why I was so sick, I should have easily managed a couple of glasses of wine. The only explanation I could think of was that I had not had any sleep for over thirty hours and had very little to eat during that time. The outcome though was surprising. I was now the chief engineers best buddy. He personally wiped the vomit from my shirt, carried me to the cab and back aboard the ship, up the gangway putting me to bed in my cabin. Go Figure!!

Before I leave behind the original deck officer line up I have a few choice items to relate which show just what an incompetent group they were. The chief officer, Neil, was without a doubt the worst excuse for an officer you could find any where. When in port it was his primary job to ensure the safe and efficient loading and discharge of cargo, which he failed miserably, see Richards Bay. While at sea he was no better. Somewhere in the mid Atlantic I went up to the bridge to take over the watch from him, upon arriving I found he was not there, in fact no one was there. Not knowing what to do I headed down one level to inform the captain, whose day cabin is right below the bridge on the starboard side and has the same floor to ceiling windows as the bridge. That is where I found the captain and the chief officer sitting with their feet up on the window ledge drinking rum and coke, and as I was a young gung ho by the book everything you had learned in navigation school was gospel take on the world kind of person, I was naturally upset at this behaviour. I can't recall my exact words but I am sure I used the "F" word more than once. They, the captain and chief, couldn't figure out why I was so pissed off. They rationalized the situation by saying that they had the same view ahead from the bridge windows as they had here in the captain's day room, so what the F was I going on about. To this day I still shake my head in amazement whenever I think about it. Another episode with the Chief officer happened when I was to take over the watch one night while we were sailing through the English Channel, probably the busiest waterway in the world, on our way to Emden, Germany. Arriving on the bridge I could see the steaming lights of dozen and dozens of ships. When taking over the watch the officer going off watch must fully inform the man coming on watch about everything and anything pertinent to your own ship, course and speed, expected course changes, operation of navigation equipment, up coming navigation marks to expect, and more, as well as the course and speed of any traffic in the immediate vicinity whether it is coming or going and if they pose a threat or not. After I stepped foot on the bridge, Neil was all set to bolt without saying a thing. I asked him to wait a minute and fill me in on the traffic situation at least. When I looked at the radar I found it was set to the 3 mile range which showed nothing in the way of targets as they were all outside of that range. When I questioned him, pointing to the lights of various ships I could plainly see, as to their courses and speeds and why was the radar set to only 3 miles, his response was that it was too confusing when he turned the radar to a higher range. In those days of radar you had to plot the movement of ships with a grease pencil on the actual radar screen to ascertain their courses and speeds and whether they were on a collision course or not. Of the dozens of ships I could see none had been plotted, which meant he did not know, nor did I, if they were on a collision course with us. I was furious, how could this incompetent fool put the ship and all our lives at risk like that. I stormed off the bridge, telling him I would be in my cabin and to give me a call when he had things figured out and was willing and able to give me a proper hand over. Now to the captain, who was more like an ostrich than a captain. Whenever something was not going to plan he would turn his head, shrug his shoulders, and walk away. The second officer is in charge of navigation and one of his chores was to keep the charts up to date. If you let this job slip it can be a huge undertaking to catch up, especially considering we carried charts for the entire world. Once a month we would receive chart updates from the British Admiralty. Usually this means adding or deleting a navigation mark, but in some areas, like the North Sea, it can mean adding a sea floor pipe line. To find the position of a new buoy they give you its latitude and longitude which you then plot on the chart, ink in the buoy with its characteristics and then make a notion on the bottom border of the chart. To speed up this process the Admiralty issued each correction with a transparent over lay which you aligned on the chart, pin pricked the location of the buoy, removed the transparency and inked in the buoy saving the time it took to plot it's position. This was a god send when it came to adding a pipe line which could snake its way across the chart for hundreds of miles, changing direction every few miles. What Walter was doing was simply stapling these transparencies to one corner of a chart and not actually making the corrections. When he had too many stapled to one corner he would start on another corner until all four corners of the chart were covered in multiple transparencies. I pointed this out to the captain, but he just shrugged his shoulders and said nothing. Walter may have been mentally challenged, but he was a friendly sort, always smiling. He was also consistently late when arriving to take over the cargo watch. He always arrived on deck staring at his Seiko wrist watch while winding the thing up. His first words were always, "what time is it"? I started telling him the time but a time that was 15 minutes or so earlier than it actually was. My theory was that if he thought it was 12:00 when it was actually 11:45 he might actually show up at 12:00. It didn't work. I guess he would find out the correct time later in the day from another source and still be late, which probably gave him the idea that his watch was not keeping very good time. One day while in harbour we had a bunch of venders come on board to sell us their local hand made products. One vendor had a display of very cheap wrist watches, some even made from old pop cans. While I was inspecting their wares, Walter sauntered by and spotted these cheap watches laid out on the deck. He then took off his nice stainless steel Seiko watch, tossed it overboard, and purchased one of the cheap watches on display.

I digress though, so back to our Richards Bay saga. We had finally taken on board our full load of coal set off around the Cape of Good Hope for Europe, but one final note, before we left Richards Bay, the chief longshoreman presented me with six bottles of beautiful South African white wine. I guess because I was the only deck officer to be seen and had worked hard to get the ship deballasted, loaded, and underway. We were initially bound for somewhere in England, but along the way the cargo had been sold, so we were re-directed to Emden, Germany. Upon arrival in Emden the first order of business was to fire the captain, the chief officer, and Walter, the second officer. I was elevated to the position of second officer. The new captain, chief officer, and third officer were very professional and a treat to work with. After we had discharged our coal, which only took about 12 hours, we sailed for Vlissingen in Holland. Now because we did not have a cargo we went to anchor where we stayed for about a month. I was stationed on the bow for the anchoring procedure, which did not go well. I had walked the anchor out and was ready to release it as soon as I got the word from the pilot over the hand held radio to let it go. When the word came we still had considerable way on the ship, so I questioned the pilot telling him we were still moving ahead at a good clip. I got a huge verbal blast of abuse from the pilot, "I am the pilot and you are just a lowly second officer and you had better do what I say or else", sort of tirade. OK, here goes, and did it ever go. I had initially let the anchor go slowly with the brake partially applied, but when the anchor hit the bottom and with the ship still moving ahead there was no stopping the chain from running out full speed ahead. The pilot was screaming into the radio for me to apply the brake which was already cranked full on, but again with the forward speed of the ship being what it was, there was no way. The brake actually caught fire. The violent running out of the chain created a huge cloud of rust in the air, so thick I could not even see the winch. I was now worried what would happen when we reached the bitter end, so I ordered everyone from the foredeck. We watched from the main deck sheltered behind one of the hatch covers when the inevitable happened and the chain came abruptly to the end where it was shackled somewhere under the anchor winch. I swear the foredeck and winch jumped up about a foot in the air. Now it was like a crack the whip thing, with the ship swinging around 180 degrees through a crowded anchorage. We finally came to a stop with the anchor cable stretched out almost parallel to the water. Now it was time to start pointing fingers. The pilot, (pilots are never wrong), blamed the whole thing on a defective brake. Being a lowly second officer I was never consulted, but knew the real cause of the fiasco.

Somewhere along the way we had picked up a riding gang. This crew of welders and pipe fitters would spend their days making repairs to the ship's structure, cutting out rusted plating or rusted piping and welding in new. This business went on while we were laid up in Vlissingen. One day I was walking along the main deck between the hatch covers, which extended above the deck about five feet. I had been walking hunched over to protect myself from a cold wet wind blowing in off the North Sea, and for some reason poked my head up above the hatch cover for a look see. The riding gang had been working on this hatch cover, so it was covered in welding slag and metal shavings. Just as I stood up a gust of wind came along and blew metal shavings into one eye. The ship had a dedicated hospital room where I enlisted the help of the new captain's wife to try and flush the meal bits and pieces from my eye. No luck. A boat was called to transport me to shore and a waiting cab to take me to a doctor. The doctor first tried a magnet to remove the shavings, again with no luck. He then had to resort to scraping my eye ball with a scalpel. An eye patch and some eye drops later and I was good to go. Since the ship was not earning money the company was not paying for a shore boat, so we were all confined on board for the duration, unless we paid for the boat out of our own pockets and in Holland this was quite expensive. So when I got a free ride ashore a lot of people came to me with their shopping lists, including the captain, a newspaper, some cigars, that sort of thing. What I didn't know and neither did the captain, was that I was expected to head immediately back to the ship after leaving the doctor. When I finally arrived back at the small boat dock several hours after leaving the doctor's office and loaded down with my purchases, I was given a royal lambasting by the shore boat's manager. I was expecting the same treatment from the captain when I arrived back on board. It was then that I learned he did not know I was supposed to return immediately and it was more his fault than mine, so no repercussions.

With our riding gang on board and our extended stay at anchor, the riding gang were working non stop to make all sorts of repairs to the ship. One issue we had been having concerned one of the coffer dams that separated the individual holds. These coffer dams or void spaces were simply an empty space placed between two holds. They were about six feet wide, stretched from one side of the ship to the other, and from the main deck down to the the tank tops of the double bottom ballast tanks. These coffer dams contained all the steel bracing that supported the walls of the cargo holds, much like the wooded framing used in house construction. One of these coffer dams kept filling up with water and the only way to pump it dry was to lower portable pumps the 90 feet down to the bottom and pump it overboard. We had speculated that the water was flooding this space when blasting the ship, either from the wing tanks located at the sides of the ship or from the double bottom tanks. If there was a break or hole somewhere in the steel work making up the ballast tanks, then as we filled these tanks, the water would also fill this coffer dam. I don't know who made the decision or how, but it was decided to have yours truly descend into the coffer dam with a radio and check for leaks while the ballast tanks were being pressed up, that is filled with water. To get to the bottom of the coffer dam one had to climb down through a man hole located in the deck on the centre line of the ship. This man hole and its ladder led to the first level, which was about ten feet down from the main deck. Then you had to work your way to the outside of the ship crawling over all kinds of steel framing, where there was another man hole and ladder leading down to the next level. In the process of crawling from midships out to the wing tanks at the side of the ship you also had to climb through two or three man hole size openings set into the vertical web framing that supported the walls of the holds. These vertical man holes were set about five feet above the floor level. Imagine staring at a hole in a wall at about eye level and barely large enough to accommodate a human body. You have to either go through head first or feet first. Head first, you have to wiggle through the opening with your hands above your head so that you can brace yourself when you land in a heap on the floor on the other side. Feet first, you have to grab a pipe or the lip of the manhole and hoist your body up, shoving your feet though and twisting around to face the opposite direction, before landing on your feet on the opposite side. I tried both methods with mixed results. Fortunately, I was young, fit, and a weighed a whole lot less than I do today. Once I had made it to the outside of the ship and climbed down to the next level, I then had to repeat these gymnastics by crawling back to midships where there was another man hole and ladder leading down to the next level. I had to repeat this trip at least nine times as a I made my way lower and lower into the bowels of the coffer dam. Why the ship's designers didn't make this descent a straight in line climb from deck level to tank top, I'll never know. Once I was finally standing on the tank top I discovered that the radio would only work if I was stand directly under the deck man hole 90 feet above my head. I then gave the engineers the go ahead to start the pumps. I could hear the water rushing into the the double bottom tanks under my feet. With these filled the water started filling the wing tanks. At that point I had moved back to the outside of the ship. As the water level in the wing tanks rose I started to climb up each level in turn, which was a very fortunate move. I must have been about half way back to the top when the wall of the wing tank just under the main deck collapsed. This sent a waterfall of water down right on top of me and, of course, filling the coffer dam, with me now trapped three or four levels down. With the radio useless I had to make a made dash back and forth and up to safety, level by level. With the last level and freedom in sight I was literally swimming through the remaining vertical web frame openings. If I hadn't started the journey up when I did I don't think I would writing this account.

After a month or more at anchor in Vlissingen we finally received word that we had a cargo. We were to sail first to Brixham England to drop off the riding gang and then proceeded to Vitoria Brazil where we would load a cargo of bulk steel bound for Taranto Italy. This was my first trip, a distance of around 6000 miles, as second/navigating officer, and I was thrilled. There is a huge amount of planning involved in such a voyage. I had to chart our course on many charts, ensuring each chart lined up with the next one in line. Then I had to measure the exact distance from start to end, if it was a straight line then it would be easy, which was never the case. The total distance was needed in order to calculate the the amount of fuel oil needed. Fuel oil is expensive so we were given only what we would need for the voyage.

In the mid eighties there was no such thing as satellite navigation. In the northern hemisphere we had Decca and Loran for coastal navigation, but out at sea and in the southern hemisphere we had to rely on celestial navigation which, if you don't mind me blowing my horn, I became good at. When a ship is in the middle of the ocean, knowing your exact position is not critical. It is only when approaching land after days and weeks at sea that it is important you must to know where you are. Celestial navigation can be very precise as long as you can see the sun, the moon, and the stars, which means clear skies with no cloud cover. Each day I would advance our position using our known heading and best guess of our speed. After 6000 miles, if you have had no opportunity for celestial navigation, your actual position could be a long way off your dead reckoning position. For that reason I plotted our course right through the middle of the Cape Verde Islands. When the islands show up on radar you can then get a precisely accurate position check. The captain didn't seem all that thrilled with my idea, but I guess I must have convinced him of the merits of the plan. As it turned out we had nice weather for the entire trip, but it was still nice to see those islands show up right on cue.

The steel ingots we were to load in Vitoria were massive, weighing hundreds of tons each and measuring maybe six feet thick and sixty feet long. They were so heavy that our own ship's cranes could not handle the weight, so a very large mobile crane was used to gently lower the ingots into the hold. I must stress that they were gently lowered the hundred feet down into our holds, because if one slipped out of the slings it would go right through the bottom of the ship without slowing down. The loading went well. We were down to our marks in no time. Looking down into the hold from on deck was a bit confusing. I was used to seeing cargo fill the entire hold from bottom to deck level, but because these ingots weighed so much, only the bottom 15 or 20 feet of hold space was filled leaving a gaping 80 feet of empty space above.

The Vitoria stevedores only worked during the day, which gave us plenty of time to go ashore. I discovered a quaint pub overlooking part of the harbour where I could relax in the sun, admire the view, and sip a martini. When I first asked my waiter for a vodka martini he looked confused and shrugged his shoulders. At first I thought it was the language difference, I didn't speak any Portuguese and he didn't speak any English. I had spotted the necessary ingredients behind the bar and pointed to a bottle of vodka and one of vermouth, but how to explain the recipe to the waiter and bar tender. After much flapping of arms I was invited behind the bar to teach the bartender on making the perfect martini, shaken not stirred, or is it the other way around. I had also found the shaker, some olives, and the correct "MASH" style martini glasses. After making my own martini I made one for the bartender. He seemed to enjoy it so much he made a second one for me free of charge. I'm quite sure that the bartender added the perfect martini to his drinks menu.

One evening I was approached by the third officer and asked to stand his watch while he went ashore for the night. No problem. I soon learned though, it was not just the third officer but almost the entire crew except the captain and his wife. It turns out someone had found the ideal brothel, night club, dinner club, and dancing with live music all rolled into one. When a patron entered this club they first passed through a room filled with girls. After choosing your girl she then became your date for the night. She accompanied you first to the bar for a cocktail or two, then into dinner, and finally onto the dance floor. When you had had your fill of dancing she took you to her home in her own car for the night. In the morning she drove you back to the ship. The total cost for the evening which included your drinks, the dinner, dancing, taxi service, and her was $50.00 US. What a bargain, the ultimate all inclusive brothel. This of course was related to me by the third officer who also added that his girl was married with two kids. When he had first entered her home, dad and the kids were watching TV. After being introduced to her family, the girl and the third officer retired to her room for the night. I guess it was a way of earring a little extra money with two kids to feed and clothe.

Leaving Vitoria we were bound for the Mediterranean and Taranto, Italy. Soon after departure we started having engine problems. The ship had two main engines coupled to a single shaft with a top speed of around 12 knots. Each main engine was equipped with a turbo charger. The problems began when both engines started backfiring through their respective turbo chargers. Each time a backfire occurred there was an explosion almost like a bomb going off, which shook the entire ship and made worse when the engines were throttled up to maintain our 12 knot cruising speed. The engineers, for what ever reason, were unable to diagnose the problem, so in order to prevent any damage to the engines we were forced to reduce speed to six knots. The big problem now was fuel. I had made my fuel estimates on a twelve knot cruising speed. Making good only six knots we were not burning as much fuel but still with the length of time needed to reach Taranto doubled we were going to run out of gas before we arrived. The other more minor problems were that we would run out of food and booze, and because we still had a few people on board who daily drank ten times more than the rest of us, the captain decided to close the bar and sell each of us a certain amount of booze from the bonded stores which we could take to our cabins and ration it out ourselves, as we saw fit. I bought a 24 flat of beer and a 26 ounce bottle of scotch. The chief engineer and the first engineer were the worst of this group, who soon drank up what ever amount of booze they had purchased. It was sad and pathetic. Both of them were walking around in a daze, twitching and sweating profusely. The first engineer, Peter from Germany, was going through the worst sort of withdrawal. He approached me on several occasions wringing his hands, sweating buckets, his eyes darting back and forth and never looking at me directly, asking me if I had any liquor I wanted to sell. At first I refused, but as time went on he became more and more agitated and looked like he was a heart beat away from Davy Jones Locker, so I relented and sold him my bottle of scotch. I think I had paid $2.50 for it, but I can't remember what he bought it for or even if I was reimbursed. I also don't recall the food being a problem. The major issue was fuel. We had to make an unscheduled stop in Augusta Sicily for enough bunker C to get us to Taranto.

Taranto was the end of the line for me. Our next trip would have been to New Orleans to load grain. I did phone Louise and ask her if I could make that trip, but her answer was, "come home now or don't come ever." OK, "I am on my way", but before leaving Taranto some of the officers took me ashore for a going away party. We happened to find a pizza restaurant that also served draft English beer and as everyone except me were from England this was going to be a night to remember. We had our pizza and a few pints of whatever sort of beer they served, however the English were just getting started. They kept ordering pint after pint until it was well after closing time. I could tell the owners were getting anxious to close up shop and head home, so in order to get us to leave they filled a huge glass demijohn carboy, the kind that holds wine, with beer, gave us a case of new pint beer mugs, and shoved us out the door. The restaurant was just across the street from the town square, where the English guys proceeded to open the case of mugs and pour everyone a pint while I set off in search of a taxi. It was well after midnight and the square and surrounding town were devoid of any signs of life, no people, no cars, and certainly no taxis. Amazingly I did manage to find us a taxi, that turned out to be a tiny Fiat 500, which on a good day would hold a maximum of four people. I think there was six of us plus the taxi driver and of course the demijohn of beer. The first order of business was to pour the driver a pint of beer. The next order of business was to cram everyone, along with the demijohn, into the taxi without spilling a drop of beer. I was seated in the front on someones lap, while holding the demijohn on my lap, with the rest of the crew crammed into the back seat. So off we went. As it was a long way back to the ship, the driver serenaded us with Italian opera sung at the top of his lungs driving with one hand and waving his mug of beer back and forth in time to the music. The guy whose lap I was sitting on was detailed to do the shifting of gears upon the shouted command of our driver. It was a good send off and I enjoyed the evening immensely.

The ship stayed tied up in Taranto for several weeks while we awaited replacement crew members. The chief engineer and first engineer were the first to leave, followed by most of the Polish crew. After a couple of weeks I was the last to depart. I first took a train to Bari, then a flight to Milan. From Milan I flew to Amsterdam where I stayed overnight. Finally flying from Amsterdam direct to Vancouver. After almost a year away from home I was met at the airport by Louise and my Mom and Dad.

One final sad note concerning the MV Sleeping Beauty. For all of my career at sea I have maintained my membership in the Hong Kong Merchant Navy Officers Guild, in fact I am now a life time member and still receive news letters, calendars, and day planners, and more recently a couple of monogramed and washable face masks. The most important reason for Guild membership, in my opinion, is that they will provide legal services in case you screw up big time, like a collision or grounding which can ruin your life. After I had been home for month or so I received a Guild news letter with a story concerning the Sleeping Beauty. While still tied up in Taranto the ship had been ranging back and forth at the dock which eventually snapped a mooring line. The broken line whipped forward killing a crew member aboard the ship secured just ahead of the Sleeping Beauty. The Sleeping Beauty's captain was arrested and thrown into an Italian prison. He was without Guild representation, so was forced to pay his legal fees out of his own pocket, which wiped out his life savings. The Sleeping Beauty was to be his final voyage before retiring.

CHAPTER 8

MV BERNIER

My next ship came in the form of another seismic vessel, the MV Bernier. The Bernier was a purpose built seismic ship registered in Sorel, Quebec. She was built by the Canadian government for Petro-Canada. The idea was that the government would give foreign aid in the form of seismic research to various developing countries around the world. As she was funded by the Canadian government she was not subject to the down turn affecting the seismic industry at large. After her launch she spent the first year of her life working the Grand Banks off the coast of Newfoundland. I had actually heard of her while working on the Edward O Vetter, as several of our seismic crew were applying for jobs with Sonic Explorations Limited, the Calgary company chosen to manage the Bernier. I was given the opportunity to apply as well. However, as I was set on getting a years worth of foreign sea time in order to write for my Master Mariners ticket I put the Bernier and Sonics Exploration on the back burner. So after my time aboard the Sleeping Beauty and then attending navigation school and writing and passing all the exams necessary for my Foreign Going masters ticket, I was ready to get back to work. I sent my resume to Sonics, was flown to Calgary for the interview, and awarded the job of second officer on board the MV Bernier.

My Journey

I joined the ship on June 16, 1986 in Karachi, Pakistan. We worked for a short time just off the coast of Pakistan before heading back to Karachi for fuel and supplies. Our survey area was in the Pemba Channel between Africa and Pemba Island. After about a month in this area we finally ended up in Nosy Be, an island off the north coast of Madagascar for my first crew change. We departed the ship late in the afternoon and were bused to a beautiful resort hotel with an amazing white sandy beach and crystal clear warm ocean waters. Most of the seismic crew and ship's crew were from Newfoundland, with just two of us from the west coast of Canada, myself and the chief engineer. I hate to stereotype, but the Newfies like to drink a lot, and the Bernier being a dry ship, their first stop, after checking in was the hotel bar. This was the offseason for the resort so for the locals it was a monetary dry time of year. As such we were the only guests that night. I don't know who organized it but it wasn't too long before a bus load of prostitutes arrived to take advantage of the situation. Before you could blink, almost every crew member had a girl on each arm. Not wanting to join the crew in their efforts to see who could out drink one another, I was enjoying a swim in the ocean and then the hotel's pool. Before the girls arrival the bar was alive with a crowd of noisy boisterous inebriated Newfies. After their arrival the bar emptied out as everyone headed for their rooms, girl or girls in tow. I was then able to enjoy a quiet beer before heading to my room and a good nights sleep. The next day was when the fun started. A bus arrived early the next morning to take us to the airport for our short flight to Kenya.

After checking in for the flight we were all milling around the departure lounge waiting to board the aircraft. There must have been around 50 or 60 people, our crew plus an equal number of other passengers. All of a sudden there was flurry of activity as a dozen army jeeps screeched to a halt outside, and began discharging gun toting soldiers who proceeded to surround the departure lounge. We were all, at gun point, made to line up single file and one by one hand our passports to the army officer in charge of this platoon. Once all the passport were collected the officer took them out to one of the waiting jeeps which had a girl sitting in the back seat. For over an hour she was presented each passport in turn, and as she looked at the pictures one by one would shake her head. It turns out that one of the crew had agreed to spend the night with this girl and then refused to pay her. So she had turned to the army for help in rectifying the situation. However, she could not identify the culprit from his picture alone. Maybe she should have had us line up and drop our pants for a more detailed inspection. The company, Sonics, employed a shore based manager whose duty it was to look after the ship and crew, such as booking flights, securing parts, shipping off the collected seismic data etc. It fell to this agent, the job of paying the prostitute, with an equal payment to the army officer in charge. I always wondered if this mangers job description now included a line concerning the reimbursement of unpaid hookers. After the payments were made the soldiers departed and we were free to board our aircraft for the flight to Nairobi.

    We had a very long layover in Nairobi, so a group of us hired a car and driver to take us on a tour of the local game park. We had placed our suitcases in the trunk of this vehicle. The dirt roads through the park were extremely dry and dusty, with our passage stirring up huge clouds of fine powdery red dust. Back at the airport when I retrieved my luggage I found it was covered in this red dust and despite the fact that it was securely closed, this dust had also permeated the interior and its contents. For months after I was still finding this red dust in pockets and folds of the clothing that was packed inside this case. Anyway, we saw several species of wild African animals, ostrich, elephant, gazelle and antelope.

From Nairobi we flew to London and possibly the worst flight I have ever taken. During our layover in Nairobi I had eaten something that did not agree with me. At first it was only a stomach ache, but shortly into the flight I started throwing up. Along with the stomach ache and vomiting I also had the worst headache one can imagine. The flight attendants were really fantastic, they moved me to a first class seat and fussed over like I was their first born. When the flight finally landed at Heathrow, after what seemed like months, I was placed in a wheel chair and taken to the airport hospital for treatment, given some fluids and medication, and made to rest. Whatever they gave me made me extremely drowsy and I fell soundly asleep. Sometime later a nurse woke me in time to catch my flight back to Canada. The suspected cause of my discomfort was put down to food poisoning, something I seem prone to and have been plagued with for a long time.

My second and last trip as second officer started back in Madagascar. We flew into the capital, Antananarivo and were bussed south to the port of Fort Dauphin on the very southern tip of Madagascar. It was lovely trip, the scenery changing gradually from tropical jungle to dry desert like terrain. Arriving in Fort Dauphin we found the Bernier lying at anchor. We were then collected by the ship's lifeboat for the trip out to the vessel. Shortly after arriving on board I was tasked with taking a couple of the seismic technicians ashore in the rubber boat to collect some important parts for the seismic recording equipment. The captain gave me a handheld radio so I could keep in touch with the ship and let him know our progress. I was supposed to stay with the rubber boat while the technicians went into town to await the arrival of the parts. The technicians were having none of this though but decided we should all adjourn to the nearest watering hole and enjoy a cool beverage while we waited. Relaxing with our beverage of choice, the captain began calling on the radio wanting an update of the situation. I was a little uncertain how to respond, so one of the technicians grabbed the radio and gave the captain a progress report, which included the fact that we were sitting on the dock in dusty very hot sunshine still waiting for the parts to arrive. In truth the parts had arrived and the messenger, who had hand carried them, was in fact sitting next to me, beer in hand. It was a lovely setting, sitting on an outdoor patio overlooking the ocean with a cool breeze, and smartly dressed waiters attending to our needs. The captain had by this time called me three or four times and as I was getting a little nervous with the situation, so it was finally decided to head back to the dock and back to the ship.

Departing Fort Dauphin we went back to work off the southern tip of Madagascar. The most memorable event for me working this slice of ocean were the whales. We were smack dab in the middle of their annual whale migration heading for the Antarctic. I have never seen so many whales in my life, they were everywhere. After completing our survey for this site we headed north towards Tanzania and the coast of Africa. Our seismic exploration took place in Pemba Channel, the channel between Tanzania and Pemba Island. We stayed there for probably one month. During this time we made a couple trips into Mombasa Kenya for supplies, food and fuel, and to send off the collected seismic data. A popular night spot for us was the Mission to Seamen for two reasons. One it was within walking distance from where the ship tied up and secondly and more important, was that it had a bar. It also had a swimming pool, but I was the only crew member who appreciated this amenity. One evening I was seated next to the captain in the mission's bar enjoying a cold beer, when the captain struck up a conversation with a gentleman seated next to him. At first I wasn't paying too much attention to the conversation, but my ears sort of perked up when I heard the captain asking this gentleman some rather crude questions concerning locating a certain type of working girl. His verbal questions were accompanied by equally crude hand gestures. As luck would have it the gentleman in question was actually the chaplain of the mission. A rather embarrassed captain then decided to beat a hasty retreat back to the ship. He was gone so fast I didn't even get to say OK or bye.

At this point I should talk a little about the Mission to Seamen now called the Mission to Seafarers. These Missions are a Christian welfare charity organization serving merchant crews and are run by a chaplain. They began in England around 1856 and operate in over 200 ports in 50 countries around the world. These missions provide practical, emotional, and spiritual support to merchant sailors. They operate through centres or clubs called Flying Angel clubs. These centres offer relaxation, refreshments, reading rooms, games rooms, a chapel, and in some cases accommodation. My favourite mission is in Hong Kong and is by far the largest centre with which I have had experience. It has an olympic size pool, a restaurant, a bar, a bowling alley, a chapel, a ball room, and accommodation. In Hong Kong where even a cheap hotel room is expensive, I was able to live at the mission for only a few dollars a day. The restaurant and the bar are also equally inexpensive. I lived there for about one month in 1984 while pounding the pavement and looking for a berth. After a hard day looking for a ship, I could come back, take a swim in the pool, enjoy a beer or two in the bar, and then have a wonderful cheap meal in the restaurant and because I was a ship's officer I was given my own room with a TV. I also met a few weird and wonderful people.

One such character I came across was a man named Richard from Belgian, no last name. Apparently, he was descended from Belgium royalty, but the family having fallen on hard times were forced to sell their title and with it their last name. One evening he took me to a licensed snake shop for a meal. He had a bowl of snake soup and a glass of snake wine, I declined the offer to join him. Richard was enjoy his soup when a lady came in suffering from what I suspect was a cold. The Chinese believe that certain parts of the snake have medicinal properties. The shop was a long narrow room with hundreds of small cupboard doors lining one wall. As I watched, the proprietor, using a long metal hook thing, extracted a very much alive cobra from one of these cubby holes and brought it out to the front counter next to where we sitting. The handler proceeded to hold the snakes head in one hand which he extended above his head. At the same time he was standing on the snakes body about half way down towards the tail so that its belly was exposed. The man behind the counter then felt down the snakes belly area until he found what he was looking for, the gall bladders. He then proceeded to make a small incision with a scalpel and extract the gall bladders, there was two of them. These he crushed into a bowl, added a splash of snake wine, and presented this horrible greenish yellow bile looking concoction to the lady with the cold, who promptly tossed it down the old hatch. I remember she paid $200 HK for this sure fire cold remedy. The snake, mean while, was shoved back into it's cubby hole until such time as another body part was called for. Or maybe he made it onto tomorrows special, snake in a bun, $2.99.

Another fellow I met was the sad case of a washed up Radio Officer. He was from England and went to sea during WW2 at the age of 16, and never went home. He finally washed up at the Hong Kong mission with little or no money and zero chance of ever going to sea again. He was in poor health and diminished brain activity from too much drink. I have never met a radio operator who was completely sane, they were all, to varying degrees, a little on the goofy side. I always put it down to all those dots and dashes of morse code rattling around between their ears. I don't know how long he had been living at the mission, probably many months. He spent his days from opening to closing, in the bar. I suspect he had run up quite the tab, so management had decided it was time for him to go. They tried to find out if he had any relatives back in England to no avail, and was packed off to a mental hospital in Kowloon. One day the chaplain came to me a told me that he was not doing very well and it might be a nice gesture if I paid him a visit and took him some cigarettes. When I found the hospital and told the staff the reason for my visit I was shown to a day room with around 15 poor souls who were all well to the left of of normal, mentally. Every single patient was doing exactly what one would expect from severely mentally challenged individuals. They were drooling, picking their noses, staring off into space, babbling nonsense, twitching, but you get the picture. I made my way over to the table where the radio operator was sitting having a conversation with the air. I sat down and handed him his cigarettes. The first thing he said was, "so they got you too". I didn't know what he was talking about, so he went on to explain that we were all part of a ship's crew who had been shanghaied. I guess I must have looked more than sceptical as he started pointing out individual crew members. He pointed at one drooling nose picker and explained that he was in fact the captain. He went around the room pointing out the twitching chief engineer, the babbling cook, the wild eyed chief officer, etc. I left Hong Kong shortly after that visit. I often wonder what happened to him.

However, I digress. After the Bernier had finished her survey in the Pemba Cannel area, we were directed to head to the Red Sea. Taking our leave of Mombasa, we had just dropped off the pilot when one of the engineers, while checking the steering gear discovered two teenage stowaways. Undocumented stowaways are a huge problem for a ship. If we had not discovered them when we did we would not have be allowed to enter our next port or any port for that matter. As we were only a mile or so offshore it was quit obvious that they could not have snuck on board anywhere else but Mombasa, so the Kenyan officials agreed to take them back. These two kids were in their early teens wearing only a ragged T-shirt and a pair of equally ragged pants held up with a bit of string. They had no shoes, no other possessions, no money, no ID, nothing. So before the pilot boat could return to pick them up we gave them a meal and rounded up a small suitcase each with donated clothing and shoes, and some cash. Months later we were tied up in Casablanca when one of these boys approached me to say hello. He was back to wearing similar ragged clothing, no shoes and no money. I didn't recognize him but he saw the ship and recognized me. He told me had stowed away on a fishing boat and ended up in Morocco, again penniless and starving. I gave him some money. Whenever we tied up alongside in African ports, we would be approached and asked when we would be sailing. If a potential stowaway was to sneak on board he wanted to do so at the last possible moment so as to minimize the risk of discovery. Our entire crew, if asked our sailing date, were told give a time and date weeks in advance of the actual date.

After leaving Kenya we set sail for the the Red Sea. Arriving in the Gulf of Suez at the northern end of the Red Sea, we commenced a very short seismic survey, lasting only a few days. The survey took place just off the Port of Suez, the southern entrance to the canal. The hard part of this survey was towing our seismic streamer across the traffic lanes leading to the assembly area for conveys traveling north through the canal. Once the north bound convoys headed into the canal we could breath only a momentary sigh of relief, as it was not long before the south bound convoys began exiting the canal, making their way into the traffic lanes leading into the Red Sea. Our seismic streamer was a cable two miles long from the stern of the ship to a tail buoy which was very difficult to see either with binoculars or on the radar. It was the job of the deck officers to try and keep ships from crossing this streamer. If a passing ship were to cross the cable too close to the tail buoy or too close astern of our ship it could severely damage this million dollar streamer. Even a ship passing somewhere in the middle of the cable risked sucking it to the surface. The cable is equipped with a number of "birds" along its length. These birds are wing like devices which can be controlled from the instrument room allowing the technicians to adjust the depth of the cable at various points along its length and keep the cable in spec, according to the parameters of the survey. These birds have been, on rare occasions, used to dive the cable in case a passing ship refuses to change course and avoid crossing the streamer. If that happens then it could take days to get the cable back in spec and hence back to work, and, as they say, time is money. So it was a very stressful few days for us playing chicken with this steady stream of ships heading either north or south. The captain was the most stressed out and could be heard and seen venting his frustrations with this difficult situation, to anyone on the bridge who would listen. Unfortunately, he did not seem to care who was present when he made his opinions known. His rants, using very colourful language, were mostly directed at the "idiots" who came up with this survey. Unbeknownst to him however, the client who was paying for the survey was one of those idiots present on the bridge. Thus this was to be the captains last voyage, he was let go at the end of this trip. It was too bad because I really liked the man and thought he was a good captain. As a result, the chief officer moved up to captain, I moved up to chief officer, and we hired a new second officer. After completing this short survey we traveled north through the Suez Canal, across the Mediterranean Sea, out through the Straits of Gibraltar, turned left, ending up in Agadir Morocco.

CHAPTER 9
M.V. BERNIER 2

I NEXT JOINED THE SHIP IN Agadir Morocco and I was now the chief officer. There is not a lot to about this time, just that we were shooting seismic off the coast of Morocco. The days all seemed to blend into one another. Shooting seismic is like driving the same stretch of highway over and over again. One event that does stick in my mind is "THE PARTY". For what ever reason, seismic workers and management the world over, love a good party. This one took place in Agadir shortly after I arrived back on board. It was held in a very nice upscale hotel in the city and was a sit down dinner for around one hundred people. The outgoing crew were held back so they could attend the festivities along with the incoming, my crew. There were also a head table of dignitaries from Petro-Canada, the owners of the ship, and Sonic Explorations, the company managing the seismic operations. Also present at the head table were several of the dignitaries wives. I have been down this road several times over the years and kind of new what to expect. It has been my experience that seismic workers in general, are a very thirsty lot and with the booze flowing like water it was not too long before 99 % of the guests, including the head table were three sheets to wind. I remember sitting next to a British gentleman who was extremely inebriated even before I sat down. The waiters had just cleared the first course of the meal and passed out the main entree. I was about to dig in when my neighbour passed out with his head face down squarely in his plate of food. That was only the opening act. I could have written the script for what followed, days in advance. These parties always seem to follow a set pattern, first comes enough liquid refreshment to float the good ship Bernier, followed by each of the dignitaries at the head table giving a presentation, which also seemed to follow a set pattern, namely what a good bunch of blokes we were and what a wonderful job we were doing. These presentations always elicit a response from some of the more lubricated of the party goers, which usually boils down to a drunken and slurred rant against anyone higher up the food chain than themselves. This is all so predictable, I'll never understand why the organizers don't curtail the flow of liquor, at least until after the presentations; but wait, this was only the opening act. There was more to come. During the presentations, with the head table loaded down with food, bottles, and glasses, one of the presenters, while giving his little ra ra speech, made a disparaging remark about one of the wives seated at the head table. This wife's husband, who was seated about 3 or 4 people to one side of this presenter, immediately jumped up and launched himself across the crowded table at the speech maker, grabbing him around the neck, wrestling him to the ground, knocking over the table, and sending everything on it crashing to the floor. I kid you not. I suppose dignitaries are not immune to the effects of excess alcohol consumption either, and if you can believe this, once the head table was back on its feet and some order restored, it was announced that we could all move into the disco with an open bar. That was enough fun for one night for me and I headed back to the ship.

And so started another two month tour of duty, finally ending up in Las Palmas Canary Islands.

Once we have reached our designated survey site, it is non stop, 24/7 until our two months are up or we finished that particular survey. These surveys were a series of grid lines along which the ship moved shooting and recording the seismic data. The survey was handed to us by the geologists and was drawn on a large sheet of paper with the precise position of each line given in latitude and longitude. This chart of the survey did not show any other features, no shore line, no depths, no bottom contours, nothing. It was our job to transfer the coordinates of these lines onto a marine chart of the area. The survey planners had a nasty habit of drawing these lines over reefs or rocks or even onto the shore line itself. A lot of times they would start or end a line right at the shore line. The seismic streamers we used were two miles long and and when in use had to be straight as an arrow behind the ship. This meant that when you started a line you had to start two miles before the actual line start in order for the streamer to be straight with no curves from a turn. This also meant you had to steam for two miles past the end of the line so the streamer's tail end is crossing the finish line in a straight line. It was a constant battle to try and explain to the planners why we were unable to finish the last two miles of a line that ended right on the shore. At this time there was no GPS we could use for navigation, so three or more stations were set up on shore to accurately fix our position in real time. We did have Satnav that used satellites in a polar orbit, but because you could only get a position fix when a particular satellite was over head it was not a precise enough method of navigation for seismic work. The information from these shore stations was received by the seismic technicians, processed and fed to a tiny 10 or 12 inch TV monitor mounted on the bridge. Besides the current ship's position in latitude and longitude, it displayed a series of three numbers. The top number was the end of line or EOL, the second was cross track error or CTE, and the last number or numbers was start of line or SOL. From looking at these series of numbers you could tell exactly where the ship was in relation to a line, and where you needed to be. Taking a line say 10 miles long, if the EOL read +5.00 then you were half way along that line. Starting that line the EOL would read +10.00 and would count down to 0.00 when you reached the end. If the number was a negative, -2.00, then you were 2 miles past the end of the line. Cross track error was also displayed in a similar fashion, +1.00 meant you were 1 mile to the right of the line, if it showed -1.00 you were to the left of the line by 1 mile. A reading 0.00 meant you were on the line. The start of line was always 0.00 so if showed any other number positive or negative you knew you were either x number of miles from the start, the finish, or past the end. To start this line you had position the ship so the numbers read, SOL -2.00, CTE 0.00, and EOL + 12.00. It all sounds very complicated, but once you got used to the idea it was no problem to visualize the ship's position in relation to any particular line.

We continued to work the west coast of Africa for the next year and four months. We had started off of the coast of Morocco in the north and worked our way south, finally finishing up in Angola. There is not a lot to talk about except for a few memorable moments here and there.

After our Morocco survey was completed, the ship was to host a party for some Moroccan dignitaries, including the King of Morocco. As security was foremost on the agenda it was decided that the entire crew must vacate the ship for the afternoon. The only crew left on board would be the captain and chief engineer. As chief officer it fell to me to round up the crew, take them ashore, and keep them amused until it was time to return to the ship. What to do with 30 odd crew for 5 or 6 hours? Not a problem. I was given a wad of

Moroccan dirhams, enough to choke a camel, in order to carry out this task. So, I marched the whole lot of them into town and into the first bar/restaurant we came across, and was large enough to accommodate them all. I then gave the bar's owner the entire wad of cash and told him to keep the boys happy and that I would be back to collect them at a certain time. I never counted how much money was in the bundle of bills I handed the owner, but it must have been substantial, as his eyes almost popped out of his head. I then spent the afternoon exploring Agadir until it was time to collect my charges. I never expected to receive any change back from the money I had handed over, but was pleasantly surprised. After rounding up the crew, the owner came to me with a fist full of receipts for every single drink or menu item consumed by the crew and then handed me back the unused portion of the money. I was blown away.

Leaving Morocco and before making our way south down the west coast of Africa, we set sail for Las Palmas, Canary Islands and a visit to the shipyard for bottom paint and other repairs. When we arrived in Las Palmas we had a few days to explore and sample the local sites and delights before the ship was hauled out. One of our more favourite attractions was a pub that featured tables and chairs set up on the sea wall overlooking a topless beach. It was a treat to be able to sit out in the sun, sample a pint of the local brew, and enjoy the view. The ship was hauled out a few days later and myself and the rest of the crew were flown home for our time off. While I was home the opposite crew had finished the refit, re-launched the ship, and sailed for the west coast of Gambia.

From March of 1987 until the end of the year we completed several major surveys primarily off the coast of Senegal and Cabinda. Cabinda is a province of but not attached to Angola. Cabinda and Angola are separated by a narrow strip of territory belonging to the Democratic Republic of the Congo. Crew changes had us flying out of the Cabinda airport to Luanda, the capital of Angola, and to Europe and home and in the opposite direction when returning from shore leave. At this time Angola was involved in a bloody civil war. One faction, the MPLA backed by Cuban soldiers with Soviet support were fighting against the anti communist UNITA backed by the USA and South Africa. Before 1975 Angola was controlled by the Portuguese and Luanda was a beautiful tropical holiday resort town. Flying into Luanda in the late eighties, what you saw looked like the pictures you see of the Ukraine today, lots of bombed out buildings with rubble blocking the streets. Coming or going, we were first flown by helicopter from the ship to the Cabinda airport or what was left of it. The airport building was nothing but a bombed out shell, so ticketing and baggage was handled out of a hanger. Our flights were arranged so when we landed in Luanda we de-plained from the Cabinda flight, walked across the tarmac and immediately boarded the flight to our next stop, either Brazaville or Paris direct. I've seen pictures of Luanda back when the Portuguese were still in power, it was a beautiful resort city with mile after mile of hotels lining the white sandy beach, looking much like pictures of Cancun you see today. I was told by someone that out of the thousands of hotel rooms available before the civil war, only 25 rooms in total were still in use in 1987.

On May the 4th, 1987 we tied up in Dakar, Senegal for our next crew change. We usually got at least one night ashore before our flights home, and the Bernier being a dry ship, the first thing everyone looked forward to, was finding the closest bar that served cold beer. As is the case the world over, the dockyard areas are tightly controlled. One needs a pass to get out and back in. So, before heading ashore, each crew member is issued a shore pass. Sometimes a customs inspector will issue these passes to the captain when he has cleared the ship to enter the country, but in this case our agent was given the task, as he had a few words to say to us all. His little speech amounted to the fact that Dakar could be very dangerous, especially at night. His advice was to always travel in a group and do not walk about alone. Fair enough, just give us our passes, we are thirsty. About 2 or 3 blocks from the docks, we found a lovely watering hole that suited our needs. I was never one for staying out too late, so after a couple pints I wanted to head back to the ship. Heeding the agents warning, I canvased each and everyone of the crew trying to find someone to walk back to the ship with me. No luck, they were just getting started. So I set off walking down the middle of the street with a very determined gate, nobody was going to stop me. I arrived back at the gates of the docks waving my pass, and congratulating myself on having made it back safely, when I was grabbed by two hulking and very black seven foot tall, mean looking and heavily armed soldiers. One under each arm they frog marched me into a nearby building. I was thinking all sorts of nasty thoughts. How will the ship know where I am? Will I miss my flight home, and stuff like that? The two guards hauled me into a room, and presented me to, what I assumed were several army officers. I was let go, they saluted, and left. One of the officers spoke a little English and asked me if I knew how to work an 8 mm move projector, which fortunately I did. They were threading the film tightly through the lens and every time they switched it on it would simply burn a hole in the film. You have to leave a loop of film above and below the lens for it to work. After I had demonstrated the correct procedure and switched the projector on, I discovered they were trying to watch a porno flick. A few back slaps later I suggested we send out for some beer, which was greeted with enthusiasm, although I was the one who had to pay for the beer. I don't remember too much about the actual movie, except for the fact that the male actor never took off his shoes and socks. I stayed long enough to drink one beer, before bidding my fellow movie patrons a good night, and making my way back to the ship. Later, it made sense to me, that the officers must have given the order to grab the first white guy that came along.

That was my last shift as chief officer. The next time back I was elevated to the lofty position of captain. Also around this time our shift schedules were changed from two months on and two months off, to two months on and one month off. This did not sit well with the crews and there was a lot of grumbling and dissatisfaction, which affected our work and the ship as a whole. While working in this area, Cabinda, we were employed by Cabinda Gulf Oil based in San Fransisco. The company had built a sizeable town called Malongo to house and care for all the workers needed to run their operation. The Cabinda oil field was huge and comprised many drill rigs, production platforms, and an anchored super tanker for crude oil storage and handling. The town had everything you would expect to find if it were situated in the USA, houses, shopping, medical facilities, and recreation facilities. They also had a fleet of helicopters that made the rounds of all the platforms and ships in the area twice a day, dropping off or picking up mail, supplies, and personnel. It seemed like over the next several months every crew member managed to wrangle a trip ashore for any number of reasons. I need to see a doctor, I need to see a dentist, or even I need a hair cut. I was the only poor sod who never got to enjoy a run ashore. I couldn't come up with a valid enough reason for the captain to leave his ship. We could also order supplies of every description to be transported out to the ship either by helicopter or crew boat. It was then that I came up with a plan to improve the morale of my crews. I was going to order a six pack of beer, once a week, for every crewman, which they had to pay for themselves. The change in the crews attitude was immediate and positive. Each crew member could elect to participate or not, there were only two people who opted out. When the suds arrived on board I had it delivered to my cabin for distribution. A lot of these seamen and seismic techs were a rough lot, going days or even weeks without bathing or shaving and wearing the same soiled and ragged clothes for weeks on end. That all changed on beer delivery day. I hardly recognized them as they lined up outside my door looking like they were attending prom night. To a man, they were bathed, clean shaven, wearing their best Sunday going to meeting clothes, and smelling like they had taken a bath in after shave. I had expected some negative feed back from Sonics, but with the huge improvement in morale and their work, I heard not a peep.

One of my last crew change out of Cabinda happened in the fall of 1987, and because of the war in Angola, was a bit unusual. As previously mentioned, one side in this civil war was backed by the Soviet Union. The Soviets did not involve any of their own troops in the conflict, but instead supplied Cuban troops. Shortly before my expected crew change, one of the Cabinda Gulf Oil helicopters was shot down by the Cuban military, killing the pilot. As a result, flights out of Cabinda were cancelled. The problem now was, how to transfer both crews, outbound and inbound, between the ship and Luanda. Sonics came up with the idea to use a fast crew boat. When I first heard about this plan I was incredulous. Their solution was to load the entire ships crew and the entire seismic crew onto a crew boat and sail it to Luanda, about a 10 hour voyage. The incoming crews would then board the same boat for the return trip to Cabinda. This would have left the ship without a crew, especially a captain and chief engineer, for an entire day. Several of the seismic personnel did not participate in the regular crew rotations, but instead stayed on board for the entire survey. These guys would then be left to man a ship at sea without any training or the necessary certificates required. I was dumfounded and naturally refused to have anything to do with this mad scheme. There was a lot of back and forth between myself and the company before I finally agreed to allow the crews to go, leaving only myself and chief engineer on board along with the 2 or 3 seismic techs to act as seamen or oilers as needed. It was still a dicey situation, but the best we could come up with at the time. The incoming crew arrived a day later. It was now time for myself and the chief to leave. We were flown by helicopter to the Cabinda airport where our chariot was waiting to take us to Luanda. There were no commercial flights flying out of Cabinda so the company chartered an executive jet for us. It was fantastic, only two passengers on a plane that could hold a dozen. It was luxurious to say the least, leather wrap around seats, a sofa, and crystal glasses in the bar, although through an oversight I'm sure, the bar was not stocked with any adult beverages. The chief and myself arrived in Luanda about an hour later, fresh as daisies, showered and shaved, and well rested only to find the rest of crew looking very much the worst for wear. They were dirty, unshaven, and tired, some of them looked as if they had just been involved in a barroom brawl. It seems their little boat ride was hell on earth, having been bounced around inside an aluminum can for 10 hours. Many of them had been sea sick. I did one more crew change into Cabinda, but by then the airport, such as it was, had re-opened.

We completed our surveys for Cabinda Gulf Oil around the end of the year, 1987, and headed back to Las Palmas for a bit of a lay up, as there was no work for us. I spent the next few months at home while the ship was tied up in Las Palmas, with only a skeleton crew left on board to look after things.

CHAPTER 10
MV BERNIER 3

I WAS ONLY HOME FOR ONE month when I had to fly back to Las Palmas. From there we sailed north into the North Sea, arriving in Den Helder, Holland. From February to December 1988 we worked all over the North Sea, from Holland to Norway. Again, it was the same old seismic game only this time we had the infamous North Sea weather with which to contend. Along with the wind and waves we also had a huge amount of marine traffic to deal with. If we were simply a ship traveling back and forth, other vessels we encountered would not pose a problem, play by the rules and all would be well. However, towing a two mile long seismic streamer behind the ship complicates the traffic situation immensely. This seismic streamer is worth, back in 1980's, in the neighbourhood of one million dollars. It is also extremely fragile, so you do not want a passing ship to come within two miles behind you. It seemed to me for every hour spent actually shooting seismic, an hour was spent repairing the streamer. This is where the bridge crew really earned their money. We were constantly on the VHF radio, calling other vessels, trying to coax them into staying well away from us and our streamer. We also used white and green flares to attract a ship's attention when all else failed. One time I had a rather dim witted second officer who had called me to the bridge when he had failed to contact a ship that was going to cross a mile astern of us. The Bernier had two radar sets. By todays standards these radars could have come over on the Mayflower. You had to bury your head in a hood and plot the movement of other vessels with a grease pencil directly on the radar's screen. If it was a sunny day you did not want to take your head out of this hood to look around, or your night vision would be compromised when you looked back. While we had our faces glued to this hood we also were able to hold the VHF's hand set to our head so we could keep trying to contact an approaching vessel. The usual methods of contact would include giving this vessel his heading or his position relative to a point of land. When the contact came closer and you could see it with a pair of binoculars, you could also describe the ship. While the second officer was plotting the target on his radar, I was doing the same on my radar. As the target got closer, I started watching it with binoculars and could make out some distinctive features of this ship that we could use to identify it. I then told the second officer, who still had his face buried in his radar hood with the VHF handset glued to his ear, to call with the information that we were trying to contact a ship with a red funnel and a white hull. The second officer immediately popped his head out of his radar and into mine and asked me how I could tell if the target had a red funnel?

We were in and out of Den Helder many times over the next few months. We all appreciated the town for several reasons. I guess the main reason was from where we tied up it was only a short 5 minute walk to the old town centre and its many pubs serving good dutch beer. It is also an old and historic place having been built when cars were not the preferred mode of transportation. The streets are narrow and winding, with not enough room to accommodate even the smallest economy car. Vehicles were not aloud in the old town. There were many quaint old pubs and we all had our favourite. I was sitting in my favourite watering hole one evening, enjoying a cold brew when I noticed several of my crew enter a coffee shop across the street. My first thought, was, "why are they going into a coffee shop when they could be in a pub drinking beer"? I still can't believe how naive I was at the time. What I didn't know was that marijuana and hashish was legal in Holland and legally sold and consumed, or smoked, in licensed coffee shops. Having finished my beer, I walked across the street to see what was attracting these crew members into a coffee shop and not a pub. It didn't take long for the penny to drop. As soon as these guys saw me they immediately tried to hide what they were up to, which was impossible as the smoke was so thick you didn't need to light up to enjoy the benefits of the drug. All you had to do was stand in the middle of the room and breath. They all hung their heads, looking very sheepish, and wondered if they were in trouble, but after the initial shock wore off, I assured them they were not, as long as they didn't bring any of it back to the ship.

The seismic operations were largely controlled by computers. These computers, state of the art in the 1980's but antiquated by todays standards, were the heart of the operation. They correlated all the data collected and matched that to the precise time and location of each line shot. When the data is analyzed by the geologists back home they can then pinpoint the actual location of any interesting sub sea formations. Without the computers it would be impossible to find the exact location of these formations months or years later. There were always minor gliches in the systems, but for the most part the seismic technicians were able to find and repair these problems. That is, until one day in the North Sea off the coast of England the system crashed big time and nothing our onboard techies could do would bring the system back to life. We were forced to call in outside help. The

Bernier was equipped with a purpose built helicopter deck, more on that later. You would think management would hire a computer specialist and fly him out to the ship and be done with it, but no, they decided, so I was told, that the helicopter option was too expensive and they would send the specialist out to the ship on a crew boat. At that time the weather was miserable, gale force winds and rough choppy seas. I don't know how long the ride out to the ship took, many hours at least, so by the time our computer man had made it out to us he had been violently sea sick for all those many hours. The poor guy was more dead than alive and had to be physically carried on board and up to his cabin, where he remained for the next several days. Now this technician was charging a lot of money for his services, from the minute he left his home ashore to the minute he got back. Any money saved by not hiring a helicopter was wasted as Sonics was now paying him hundreds of dollars an hour to lie in his bunk vowing never to set foot on a boat again.

Speaking about the helicopter deck, the ship was built with a standard approved and designed deck, not something that was added later as an after thought. Once we started on a survey the ship worked 24 hours a day, seven days a week until completion. Thus this helicopter deck was essential for everything from crew changes to shipping the collected data ashore. As I mentioned, when working for Cabinda Gulf Oil, off of the west coast of Africa, we had two helicopters a day land and take off from this deck for an entire year. Suffice it to say we were not amateurs when it came to dealing with these daily helicopter visits. After we arrived in the North sea we were surprised to learn that the British would have to inspect and approve our ship before any future helicopters would be allowed to land. Two inspectors were then duly dispatched via crew boat to carry out this inspection. They cited us for two faults. The first was that we were not using a cargo net stretched across the deck for the choppers to and on. I think the theory was that with metal to metal contact between the aluminum landing skids of the chopper and the steel deck there was the potential for the helicopter to skid across the deck as the ship rolled from side to side. The ropes of the cargo net were there to provide some form of resistance in the event the ship rolls. In theory maybe, but in practice the net made for a highly dangerous situation. The net was made from roughly 1/2 inch diameter hemp ropes and was comprised of about 6 to 8 inch squares. It was meant to be stretched flat across the deck from side to side and from forward to aft and secured around the perimeter. The problem was the down wash from the helicopters spinning blades would allow the net to flutter up and down and then become entangled in the landing skids of the helicopter so that when the pilot attempted to take off he would be anchored to the deck by one end of one landing skid. This would cause the helicopter to tilt up every where except the one point where it was caught in the net, and could lead to the spinning blades contacting the deck and making a real mess of things. Some of us, I was one, had to undergo training in safe helicopter procedures and what to do in the case of a mishap. We watched all sorts of training films depicting accidents, what to expect, and what to do about them. Prominent among these films were images of landing skids caught in cargo nets and the resulting accidents, some of them fatal. However these inspectors still insisted we make use of the cargo net. Actually this ruling did not last long, there was a fatality of this type somewhere else in the North Sea and we received a warning to discontinue the use of cargo nets immediately. The second infraction we were cited for was the large H painted on the deck. Our H was oriented with the H facing fore and aft. This was, apparently, was not the correct way for painting an H on a helicopter deck. It must be oriented from side to side or 90 degrees form the fore and aft line. If you ask me, these inspectors had to find some fault in order to justify their jobs.

After working the southern portions of the North Sea, we moved north off the coast of Norway where we spent the next six months. The ports of call we visited were Stavanger, Kristiansund, and Bergen. There is not a lot to write about for this period, same old seismic stuff. Norway looks a lot like the west coast of British Columbia, with its rocky tree lined deep fiords. I felt right at home. The only thing that put me off was the Norwegian beer. It was horrible stuff and gave me violent headaches after drinking only a small glass. If I did go out to a pub I always asked for an imported brew. Norway is, or was at the time a very expensive place. Even though the local brew was much cheaper, I was forced to go for the more expensive imports. I remember once paying the equivalent of $15 Canadian for one bottle of Dutch beer, and this was back in 1988.

Another port we called into was Aberdeen in Scotland. When a ship enters a foreign port they always take on a pilot who has local knowledge and knows where to go. Aberdeen was no exception. However, on this occasion I could smell the pilot before I actually met him. He had a large very red nose lined with prominent veins, the sure sign of a heavy drinker, and smelled like he had just taken a bath in scotch whiskey. Aberdeen harbour is a maze of docks and basins, so I needed the pilot to at least show me the way and where we were to tie up. Having a pilot on board does not relieve the master of his duties as captain of a ship. The catch phrase is, "to master's orders and pilots advice". I was keeping a very close eye on this pilot and had even countermanded a few of his helm orders to the seaman steering the ship. This was alright as long as we had lots of sea room around us, so I let the pilot continue our journey into the harbour. However, when we entered the narrow opening to our assigned dock I could see he was going to make a cockup of the landing, and as a result, I told him that I would take it from here and he was free to leave. I don't think I raised my voice that much, but my words to the effect, "get off my bridge" had their desired affect and he scurried off with his tail tucked between his legs. The best part of a night ashore in Scotland was I got to sample some very fine whiskeys which were a whole lot cheaper than Norwegian beer.

I think it was our last trip heading south and back to Den Helder when we passed an oil platform off the coast of Scotland which had just exploded in a huge ball of fire. The platform was named Piper Alpha. The burning platform was surrounded by dozens of support ships either fighting the fire or attempting to rescue survivors. There was nothing we could do to help except stay out of the way and pray for people involved. It was the worst oil field disaster in the history of the north Sea. It finally claimed the lives of 165 men.

The Bernier was built in Quebec by the Canadian government for Petro-Canada. The idea was that Canada would give foreign aid to developing counties in the form of seismic research. I think it was for a five year term, which ran out around the time we had finished the Moroccan survey. For the next year or so, Sonics was allowed to manage the ship until it could be sold. This allowed Sonics Exploration to pursue private contracts, which started with Cabinda Gulf Oil and with us ending up in the North Sea. We all knew the ship would be sold at some point, which happened in December 1988, on our final trip into Den Helder. The buyers were Duke University, Durham North Carolina, USA. Before leaving Holland for the trip across the pond to deliver the ship to her new owners, we first had to be dry-docked. There was a couple of reason for the haul out, the most important was, so that a survey could be done of the underwater portion of the hull. The second reason was, for the installation of a series of transducers along the length of the hull from bow to stern. These transducers are simply underwater microphones. The idea was to find the quietest part of the hull. Too close to the bow and the noise of the bow wave would interfere with and cause excess noise on recordings from that sensor. Too close to the stern and the noise of the propeller would likewise cause interference. In order to monitor these transducer during the voyage west, two technicians from the university would accompany us. These two guys were your typical geek tech savvy electronic experts. They were given space in the instrument room for this monitoring and recording task. Before our departure I was making the rounds of the ship in order to make sure everything was in order, equipment stowed and secured etc, when I noticed the two techs had placed their electronics on a table without securing them in any way. After all, we are heading out into the North Atlantic in the middle of winter. I told these techs they were going to have fasten there equipment down securely or it would be on the deck in bits and pieces in no time at all. They both gave me quizzical looks, not understanding a ship actually rolls around at sea. I think this was the first time they had even seen the ocean, let alone set foot on a boat of any kind. A few hours later I came back to check on them to find they had used duct tape to secure the equipment to the table. They had stuck the tape to one side of the table, stretched it up and over the electronics and down to the opposite side of the table. One strand only. Not good enough, so I had one of the seaman give them a hand in securing their equipment. One of these techs asked me to inform them when the sea state was force three, (7 to 10 knots of wind) or less, so they could do their research. Remember, this is mid December and we are heading across the North Atlantic to the east coast of the

USA. I told them they had better do their research right now, before we leave.

This voyage turned out to be the worst in all my years at sea. We were not even out of the English Channel when the sea state went from 6, to 7, to 8, and even 9. We tried everything we could to evade the worst of the weather, all to no avail. Probably around mid Atlantic we were finally hove to, using just enough engine power to hold our head into the wind and waves. That was when we received a mayday call. At this point we were holding on only by the skin of our teeth, how in the name of all that is holy were we going to be able to respond to a mayday. The call had come from an ocean going Smit Lloyd tug, named the Smit London, who's position turned out to be only 50 miles away. These large tugs are extremely strong capable vessels and much more likely to survive the weather than one little flimsy seismic boat. In any case, it was flatly impossible for us move even 10 miles in their direction, let alone 50 miles. After contacting the tug we learned that it was not them in need of assistance, but the crew of jack-up oil drilling platform, the Rowan Gorilla, they had been towing, which had capsized and sunk. The jack-up's 27 man crew had abandoned the rig and were being tossed around in a life capsule. The captain of the Smit London was recording winds of 60 to 70 knots and wave heights of 50 to 60 feet and was concerned that the life capsule would not survive the stormy conditions. At one point he had witnessed the capsule engulfed by a 60 wave. Fearing the worst he had even written in his log, "they are gone". The next day the Smit London was able to launch a rescue craft and retrieve the very sea sick crew. At the same time we were having our own problems dealing with the weather. In our galley we had a huge stand alone walk in fridge. This fridge was a stainless steel cube maybe 15 feet on a side and 8 feet tall. It had been bolted down using some very flimsy brackets welded to the deck. These brackets had broken free and the fridge was now madly waltzing around the galley smashing everything in sight. To corral this monster we assembled a crew armed with ropes and lengths of timber. We would wait outside the galley door until the ship rolled away from us and the fridge slid across the deck allowing us to charge into the galley and hopefully secure the thing before the ship rolled back the other way, threatening to squash us. It took several attempts but we finally managed get the thing under control. Finally, after what seemed like weeks, but in fact was only a few days, we were able to get underway and resume our voyage west.

We arrived in Fall River, Massachusetts, home of Lizzy Borden, around the twentieth of December, 1988. The first people ashore were the two university technicians, both of whom, after stepping off the gangway, knelt down and kissed the ground. I don't know how much work they accomplished during the trip, they seemed to have spent the entire crossing on the bridge wearing lifejackets and staring transfixed out the windows at the ugly sea conditions. After kissing the ground, they scurried off somewhere and I thought we had seen the last of them. I was wrong. They returned an hour later with enough pizza and soft drinks for the entire crew. At this point in time, most of the crew were sent home, leaving only about six of us to complete the handover to the new owners.

One person who was left behind was the Petro-Canada representative. It took about two weeks to complete the transfer. Once complete the Petro guy decides he is going to take us out for dinner. If you thought seismic people loved a good party, then next in line would be Petro-Canada staff. There was only six of us attending this dinner, myself and a deck hand, the chief engineer and an oiler, the Sonics rep and our host, the Petro guy. Our host was going to make this dinner one to remember by ordering huge quantities of liquor, from cocktails, to wine, and finally a table full of brandy. By the time the brandy arrived I was wondering how I could leave gracefully. I didn't have long to wait. The chief engineer had long held a grudge against the Petro man which finally erupted when the chief lunged across the table, grabbing Mr. Petro around the throat, and of course knocking over the table and sending all that booze to the floor. That was my cue. I was up and out of the restaurant before the last glass of brandy had hit the floor. I waited outside on the street for a bit to see what would happen. The rest of the dinner party was soon ejected from the restaurant. While walking back to the hotel the Petro rep discovered he was missing his wallet and wanted to go back. I decided to accompany him and everyone else as they were so drunk I feared they might not find their way back to the hotel safely. We all waited out on the street as he went back inside to retrieve his wallet. A short time later he came back outside, and told us he had patched things up with the restaurant and that we were all welcome to come back inside. You've got to be kidding. I had finally had enough for one night and elected to walk back to the hotel alone. The next morning, while waiting in the hotel lobby to check out, the chief engineer, who had been as drunk as one could get and still stand up, stumbled out of the elevator, looking very much the worst for wear. Thinking, he may not remember everything that had transpired last night, I told him about his assault on the Petro rep. I figured he would be full of shame and regret for his actions, but no, all he said was that it served him right.

After checking out of our hotel we were driven to the Boston airport for a flight to Halifax, so ending the story of the good ship MV Bernier. As of 2022 the Bernier is still shooting seismic. She has changed owners and names several times but recent pictures show her pretty much unchanged from when I last saw her in 1988.

One final note concerning working for Sonics Exploration and offshore oil. For some reason, the Canadian government in all their wisdom had decided that off shore oil workers did not have to pay Federal income tax. When Sonics issued my pay checks the income tax was duly deducted each month. Then when I filled my income tax return I would get a refund for all that deducted income tax. In fact, I would get back more money than had been deducted in the first place. The feds, knowing I was getting it back, payed me interest on all the funds deducted for that year. My last income tax refund check, after leaving Sonics, bought me a brand new 1989 Ford F 150 pick up truck with money left over. Fantastic!

M.V. Edward O Vetter, alongside Dutch Harbour, Alaska

Bangladesh Street Kids

M.V. Sleeping Beauty, Bar Scene
(author centre no shirt)

CHAPTER 11
MV PROBE RESEARCHER

Arriving in Halifax, Nova Scotia, I was picked up from the airport and taken to my new ship, the MV Probe Researcher. We eventually came to refer to her, not so affectionately as the Anal Probe. I knew about this new assignment but had many misgivings and had tried desperately to get out of it. I had initially refused, stating my reasons, but to no avail. Sonics brushed aside my excuses and countered with an offer that addressed all my concerns. The main issue was time off. I had been working two months on one month off for the last year or so, ever since Petro-Canada had pulled the plug, and was tired of being away from home so much. Even though one month off seemed a descent amount of time, in practice it never worked out that way. For the last year I had been getting only 3 weeks leave before having to return to the ship. One of my demands from Sonics was for a two month on two month off rotation, which they agreed to. So I was the only person among the entire ship's company getting two months off, everyone else was stuck with the one month off. Sonics also sweetened the pot, salary wise.

A little back ground on the delightful Probe Researcher. The ship was originally built as a British deep sea trawler, fishing the Atlantic Ocean around Iceland. Then came the

Icelandic cod wars of the 60's and 70's. In an effort to protect the fish stocks from over fishing, Iceland moved to extend its territorial boundaries from 4 miles to 12 miles. This sparked the first cod war. They then pushed the boundary from 12 to 50 miles and the second cod war was born. Finally, they expanded the limit from 50 to 200 miles, the third cod war. This, of course, did not sit too well with the British, who had been fishing these waters for over 500 years. There were many clashes between the British trawlers, sometimes escorted by Royal Navy ships, and the Icelandic coast guard vessels. It even came down to the two sides trading gun fire. As a result, our illustrious Probe Researcher had been fitted with some kind of naval gun on the foredeck. You could still see the old gun mountings when I joined the ship. When Iceland imposed the 200 mile limit it put a lot of British fishermen and their ships out of work. I assume that was the case with the Probe Researcher. The ship was bought by an unknown Canadian company, converted to a seismic vessel, and registered in St Johns, Newfoundland. This initial effort did not last long, the vessel was subsequently laid up in Halifax, and put up for sale sometime in the early 80's. Around 1985 I was looking to further my employment options, which took the form of an oil tanker endorsement certificate. The only school, at that time, offering this course was in Halifax. I flew to Halifax, attended the school, and added this endorsement to my resume. While in Halifax someone took me on a tour of ships in the harbour, one of them being the Probe Researcher. We got a chance to talk to the guy who was looking after the ship and even got a tour. Little did I know that years later I would wind up as her captain.

Around late 1988 the ship was put up for auction to the highest bidder. The winning bid was a university professor from the US who wanted to prove his theory on how Africa was formed, using seismic research. As the story goes, he paid $60,000.00 for her using his American Express card for payment. After setting foot on board the Probe Researcher in January 1988 for the second time, I found her to be in a terrible state. She was dirty inside and out, with peeling paint and rust everywhere. Machinery was broken or missing all together. It turned out that the caretaker, who I had met years earlier, had not been paid for his services, so had started removing equipment and selling it to recover his lost wages. Somehow I was expected to get this derelict up and running and get her to the west coast of Africa. What could possibly go wrong?

As part of the conversion from a fishing trawler to a seismic ship, she had been fitted with two enormous booms attached to the hull at deck level, one on either side. These hinged booms were attached to the hull about one third of the way aft of the bow. The idea was to swing these booms out 90 degree to the centre line of the ship in order to increase the spread of the guns. Earlier seismic ships used only two gun arrays deployed out the stern, one to port and the other to starboard. It was later found that by spreading these gun arrays out and away from the ship, it would give the seismic recordings a 3D like effect. To accomplish this, hinged booms could be swung out and away from the side of the ship with the gun arrays attached at the outer end of these booms. The Bernier used four gun arrays, two directly behind the ship and two on booms extending out either side. The Bernier's booms were only about thirty feet long. The Probe Researcher's booms were a massive, about one hundred and fifty feet long. These booms were made out of aluminum, boxed shaped, about four feet square where they attached to the ships side and tapering out to maybe two feet square at the outer ends. To support the outer ends of the booms, a wire rope tackle was led up to the top of a foremast. My concerns were the added weight of these booms, not only added at deck level, but when swung out and topped, some of this weight would then be transferred to the top of the mast. My other concern was that Sonics had welded two steel shipping containers to the main deck between the aft superstructure and the forecastle, which they promptly filled with all manner of heavy equipment, including the seismic streamer. I'm not sure now how much this streamer weighed, but I would guess a couple of tons.

Back when I was attending navigation school, one of the subjects for my Master's Certificate, was ship stability. This was my favourite subject. I even programmed a hand held computer I had, to make these stability calculations for me. All I had to do was input the various weights involved, fuel oil, fresh water, and ballast water to name a few, and the program would give me the centre of buoyancy, the centre of gravity, and the metacentric height. I use to make these calculations for the MV Bernier on a regular basis for different conditions of loading. Because the Bernier was a purpose built seismic ship there were never any issues with these calculations. However, the Probe Researcher was designed and built as a fishing trawler. During her conversion to a seismic vessel I don't think any consideration was ever given to these added weights which were all placed well above the centre of gravity. To make matters worse, the area under the main deck where these containers were installed had been a fish hold, which could conceivably hold tons of fish. This fish hold had now been converted to crew accommodation with thin, flimsy plywood panels sectioning off spaces for individual cabins. I'm sure the crews occupying this space would weigh more than wood used in these partitions, bunks, and wardrobes.

I spent a lot of time going over the the entire ship, measuring the depth of the double bottom tanks, checking the capacities of fuel oil and fresh water tanks, calculating various weights, measuring the distance above the keel for these weights, and on and on. Having made my calculations and checking them many times, I found that with all the ballast tanks, fuel tanks, and water tanks full we were just barely able to maintain a very small margin of positive buoyancy. Use up any fuel or fresh water and the centre of gravity would rise above the centre of buoyancy and over we would go. Compound this with the winter conditions we were experiencing at that time, which could lead to an accumulation of ice on the rigging and superstructure, all the fuel oil and water in the world would not prevent the ship turning turtle.

So I presented my findings to management, at first they were dismissed. The crews all knew of my calculations and the resulting stability issues with the ship. When I persisted, Sonics tried to offer some band-aid solutions, one of which was, as the fuel oil was used up it would be replaced by sea water. I don't think so. The seismic crew, all from the Bernier, had been on board for a couple of weeks before I joined ship so had time to realize the condition of the ship and the conditions in which they were expected to live and work. When they found out management were not addressing the stability issues, a couple of them walked off, never to be seen again. In fact, I fully expected to be given my walking papers. However, giving Sonics their due, they agreed to hire a firm of naval architects to validate my findings. The next day a team of six guys, all with advanced degrees from prestigious universities, descended on the ship armed with calculators, slide rules, and tape measures. I was a little unsure of myself at that point. I mean here I was, a lowly captain with a two week course in ship stability under my belt, being compared to six university graduates, with probably years of experience. All I could think of was, if I am wrong maybe they will send me home. That was not to be though. The architects calculations mirrored my own right down to the decimal points. They even invited me to their office for coffee and donuts. I was vindicated. Now the problem becomes, what to do about this situation.

The ship did have double bottom ballast tanks, but these were not nearly large enough to hold the volume of water needed to counteract the large amount of weight added so high up in the vessel. We did a calculation for filling these tanks with concrete, but even that was not enough. These ballast tanks were only about three feet from the bottom hull plates to the deck above. So, we did another calculation for filling the tanks with pig iron ballast, which proved successful. These "pigs" were ingots of cast iron and probably weighed at least 100 pounds each, or more. When we first opened up the man hole covers into the ballast tanks we found they were half filled with a thick black gluey muddy sludge, which first had to be removed. We hired a bunch of guys to crawl into the tanks and using buckets and dust pans, remove this material, one bucket at a time. It was a horrendous job and not one I would wish on my worst enemy. They did it all without complaining. Once all these tanks were cleaned these same guys then had to hand bomb thousands of iron ingots into the same tanks, all the while crawling on their hands and knees over framing and piping in sub zero temperatures. I hope they were well paid. While all this work was going on, I continued to get dirty looks from management. I still expected to be told my services were no longer required.

One of the people who had been continually harassing me from the moment I stepped on board was the party chief. This guy is hired as a manager of the seismic operations. A seismic ship has two distinct crews, the ships crew headed by the captain, and the seismic crew headed by the party chief. A similar situation exists on drilling platforms, where the tool pusher is in overall charge of the drill crew, and the captain is in overall charge of ship's crew and on paper at least in charge of the safety of the both crews. It has been my experience that on the whole tool pushers and party chiefs feel they are in overall charge of both crews and the captain, or the manager in the case of a drilling rig, is little more than a figure head put there by government regulations just to make their lives difficult. A seismic ship is different from a drilling rig in that the ship is always on the move and needs a ships crew to handle this movement. On the other hand, a drilling rig is only on the move from one drill site to the next, where once it has been anchored or jacked into position it will remain for months or even years. This leaves the rigs captain, his officers, and seamen little to do except conduct safety drills. I feel this difference is what has lead to the tool pushers and party chiefs attitude regarding a ships crew. Their jobs, either drilling or exploring, because that is the whole purpose of the venture, take precedent over everything else. This attitude is much more pronounced on drilling rigs verses seismic ships, and for me, at least, has not been too much of an issue, that is until I ran into the party chief from hell!

Before Sonics Explorations won the contract with Petro-Canada to manage the Bernier, they had been exclusively a land based seismic company. When Sonics took on the Petro-Canada project they hired a party chief out of Norway, who supposedly came highly recommended. Recommended or not, he proved to be an over weight alcoholic bully, who tried to have me fired, for unknown reasons, after serving only about two weeks as the Bernier's second officer. I didn't find this out until years later. Fortunately, several members of the seismic crew, whom I had worked with on the Edward O Vetter, came to my defence. After the Bernier was sold, Sonics severed all ties with this man and hired a party chief from their land based operations for the Probe Researcher surveys. This new guy proved to be a hundred times worse than the Norwegian party chief, with whom I had finally established a working relationship. This new party chief thought of himself as a super action hero, who if needed, would gladly sacrifice himself or members of his crew for the cause. He liked to tell stories of how macho he was by showing off his scars with tales of all the life threatening tropical diseases he had endured and over come. It was a badge of honour with him, and if you didn't have tales of suffering of your own, you were looked down upon as not being worthy. Top this off with the fact that, being land based, he had always been the top dog with no one else in sight making decisions that might affect his seismic operation. It therefore came as a very rude awakening for him when faced with a captain and ships crew over whom he had no control. To say he didn't like me was a gross understatement. He hated my guts. He wanted to manage every aspect of running the ship, from installing radio equipment on the bridge to the setting the hours of my watch keeping officers and seamen. I tried on multiple occasions to politely explain how, as duly licensed seafarers by the government of Canada, myself and my crew were legally in charge of all ship board operations. This, of course, did not sit well with him. He took to loudly letting management know what a complete idiot I was and how he could do a much better job. Then the stability issues came up and he was off. He didn't believe either myself or the firm of naval architects. He wanted Sonics to top off the fuel tanks, load up on groceries, and we would sail with the morning tide. Fortunately, no one listened to him.

After the ballasting operation was completed we immediately made plans to depart Halifax, next stop west Africa. I can't remember if that destination was changed before or after we departed. In any case, we were told to head for Bermuda and lay up, until some monetary issues with the client could be sorted out. I was still worried about icing so after monitoring the weather situation for a day or two and getting a favourable forecast for the next two days we left Halifax. These two days would allow us time to clear the Canadian coast and sail into the gulf stream. The trip was uneventful for the most part, except for some torrential rain showers along the way. The rain resulted in us discovering many leaks in the wheelhouse roof, with water dripping all over the electronics, which we had to cover with tarps. Arriving off Bermuda we tried to arrange for a pilot to take us into St. Georges harbour, but we were told that there was no pilot available at this time and we could enter the harbour on our own and go to anchor, or cruise around all night until the next day. I chose to head in on our own, which is a decision I would not make a second time. The entry into the harbour is very narrow, with several large course alterations. In order to keep the ship on track and between the marker buoys, it was absolutely imperative we not deviate even one degree from our heading. It was a white knuckle passage. Fortunately, I had a very capable seaman on the helm. After entering the harbour and dropping anchor someone suggested we lower the lifeboat and take the off duty crew ashore for some liquid refreshment. To this day, I don't know how I got away with it. I don't think we had cleared customs and immigration, which would have made this little venture illegal. Anyway, I loaded up the life boat and motored ashore. I dropped everyone off at the nearest landing and headed back to the ship, but not before telling everyone I would be back at midnight to pick them up. This lifeboat was equipped with a one cylinder high compression Lister diesel engine. While waiting for the crew to wander back to the dock I shut down this noisy smelling mechanical monster. When everyone was back in the boat, I began the process of starting the engine, which consisted of hand cranking it over with the compression release off. After several revolutions I moved the compassion release to on, only to have the engine back fire. This caused the cranking handle to violently rotate backwards and strike me in the right arm, breaking it. At the time I didn't know I had broken the bones. I just thought I was going to end up with some bruising. That thought didn't last long, I woke up the next morning with my arm swollen to almost the same size as my thigh. Something is not right here. I walked over to our agents office and asked them if it was possible to see a doctor. One look at my arm and I was rushed to the local hospital for x-rays and the fitting of a cast. The x-rays showed that I had broken both the radius and the ulna bones.

For the next couple of weeks, while Sonics and the client sorted out their money problems, I roamed the island from one end to the other. I was able to visit all the historical sites, from the Royal Naval Dockyard at the west end of the island, to Hamilton about mid island, to St George's where we were tied up at the east end. It was wonderfully warm and sunny, a far cry from the sub zero temperatures of Halifax. A paid holiday. Then it was time for me to fly home. My chief officer would eventually sail the ship across the Atlantic to Gabon, West Africa. I stayed home for two months while my broken bones healed. It was a long process of healing. My cast was cut off at one point, the arm was x-rayed which determined the it was not fully healed, and another cast fitted. For many years after the injury, I still experienced some pain and weakness in the arm.

CHAPTER 12
PROBE RESEARCHER 2

AFTER TWO MONTHS OF R AND R at home, I re-joined the Probe Researcher in Port Gentil, Gabon, West Africa, but the writing was on the wall. There were several factors involved in the eventual downfall of this venture. The biggest of these was, money. I don't think the good professor realized how much it cost to run a ship with a 30 plus man crew. On top of that was the condition of the ship and her seismic gear. There were daily breakdowns in everything from machinery to the streamer itself. These seismic streamers are quite delicate and very costly. It is basically a flexible clear plastic tube about six inches in diameter filled with hydra phones, compasses, depth sensors, and lots and lots of small fine wires. This tube is filled with a petroleum distillate called ISOPAR. This is to keep salt water from shorting out the electronics buried in the cable. However, if the cables skin is damaged admitting sea water, which is very common occurrence, the streamer must then be hauled back on board for repairs. Our particular streamer had seen better days, so the seismic crew were constantly having to repair cracks and breaks in the cable. Looking at it, I think you could see more patches than the original plastic skin. After a month or more with all the break downs we had not shot any useful data. The end was near.

There was an exciting moment for us one day when we received a mayday call from a cargo ship which had run aground on Pagalu Island, now known as Annolon Island. We were not too far away so we were the first to respond. When we arrived on scene we found a small cargo vessel loaded top to bottom with mahogany logs. The ship had run smack into the the island head on and was seemingly stuck. Most of the crew were already in the lifeboat with all their personal effects packed and waiting to be rescued. I smelt a rat almost immediately. The part of the island where the ship hit was very steep to, no beach or offshore shallows. You could literally step off the rocks into a thousands fathoms of water. The captan told me the ship was making water in a number of holds and the engine room was flooded. This did not make sense, and let's not forget this ship was loaded with logs, in the holds and stacked on deck to the height of the bridge. There was literally a thousand fathoms of water under the engine room, so how can it be flooded. Likewise, there was enough water under 99% of the ships length to fit the Statue of Liberty many times over. The only thing wrong with the ship was her bow was a little bit bent and buckled. The captan was adamant though, she was going down and they needed immediate rescue. I had been in touch with Sonics and told them of the situation. There was a very brief discussion of attaching a tow line and attempting to pull her off. This, however, was quickly dismissed. If we had attempted this risky manoeuvre and the ship did sink, then we would be held liable. So with the ship's crew on board and her lifeboat in tow we headed for Port Gentil. Waiting for us upon arrival were a contingent of local police who promptly arrested the captan and chief engineer. A tug had also been sent out to tow the ship off the island and into Port Gentil. She arrived a few days later, sporting a crumpled bow and listing some from the flooded engine room, but other wise undamaged. She remained at anchor for as long as we were in the area and I suspect long after we had departed.

Following the Pagalu Island incident we continued to make every effort to shoot some useful seismic, but it never happened. After about a month of desperately trying, dealing with broken machinery, and patching and re-patching the out of date streamer we were sent to anchor in Port Gentil. This anchorage was the last stop for broken down oil exploration ships and rigs that had far exceeded their useful life span. Some of these old drill rigs looked like they had been there for many years and were just waiting for a chance to sink beneath the waves. In fact there were the tops of several mast and derricks barely poking their heads above the oceans surface. I suppose it was a fitting place for the poor old Probe Researcher. We spent a week or two here twiddling our thumbs and not much else. We were, though, able to take the rubber boat ashore and explore the nearby area. One of the more interesting sights was a large public market that sold everything one could imagine and then some. There were long concrete tables where the vendors could rent space to display their wares. In the grocery section I noticed what looked like neatly stacked rounds of cordwood about a foot in diameter and maybe two feet long. As I got closer I realized it was not rounds of firewood but sections of a very large snake; "Yummy"! A little further along I came across, what at first looked like the burnt and blackened remains of a human baby. It turned out to be a whole smoked monkey; "Double Yummy"! We had heard that a local delicacy was monkey brains, although thankfully I was not able to confirm this rumour. If anything these wonderful gastronomic delights only strengthened my resolve to remain a vegetarian.

After our stay at anchor we were told to sail for Douala in Cameroon. For some reason we had to set sail immediately but not expected to arrive in Douala for several days. As it was only a few hours sail from Port Gentil to Douala we had time to kill. Even steaming as slow as possible we would still arrive off Cameroon a day too soon. So I decided we should visit the island of Fernando Po, now called Bioko Island. We did a circumnavigation of the island marvelling at the old Spanish style architecture of one of its major towns, Malabo. The southern end of the island is a science reserve and very lightly populated. It also boasted beautiful black sand beaches. With still more time to kill, we launched the rubber boat and took turns going ashore for a swim and to walk on the black sand. This activity was highly illegal and could have resulted in severe penalties for myself and the ship. This sort of thing would or could not happen today, but the 1980's were a different time. It was nearing our scheduled arrival time so we sailed for the approaches to Douala, picked up our pilot and finally tied up alongside. I think I only spent one night in Douala before catching a flight for home. That was the last time I ever saw the old Probe Researcher. The ship was sold to a deep sea diving company. So ended my years of employment with Sonics Exploration Ltd. of Calgary Alberta.

Before I go, there were a few more interesting events that took place off the west coast of Africa. The first one happened when the Bernier first arrived in the Cabinda oil fields. At the time Angola was involved in a long and bloody civil war. On one side in this war were Russian backed Cuban soldiers. We had just started our first survey, when a Cuban gun boat pulled alongside and ordered us to stop immediately. Our streamer was fully deployed, so we could not stop. Stopping our ship would allow the streamer to sink and tangle itself in an unrecoverable mess. Also the pressure exerted on the this fragile cable would damage it beyond repair. We tried to explain over the radio that we could not stop until we had recovered the streamer which would take several hours. In desperation the captain, I was chief officer at the time, sent me away in the rescue boat with a fistful of permits and documentation, to prove we had every right to be in the and area doing what we were doing. At first I thought, what fun going for a boat ride. My happy thoughts did not last long though. As soon as I pulled up alongside the gun boat, three very large, very black, very mean looking armed to the teeth soldiers jumped into the rescue boat. They ignored the official documents I tried to show them and instead while pointing their evil looking rifles at me, ordered me to return to the Bernier. OK, no problem. Upon returning to the ship I escorted them up to the captains cabin. I was waiting on the bridge for some sort of resolution to this situation, when the captain called up and told me I could now return the soldiers to their gun boat. And just how did the captain resolve the situation you may ask? The answer was, two cases of coke cola, one carton of cigarettes, and half a dozen bars of soap. Works every time. I had learned early on when flying in or out of these African countries you do not travel with anything valuable in your luggage or the border guards would simply confiscate it. Things like cameras or radios or money, especially money. I used to put any cash I had in my underwear. Some of us tried putting money in their shoes but when one guy was ordered to remove his shoes and the money seized by the border guards, underwear became the preferred place of concealment. I routinely would place several packs of cigarettes and few bars of soap in my suitcase. As soon as the border guards opened my luggage they would scoop up the cigarettes and soap, close my suitcase and look no further. In many cases the departure areas of the airports were a mad house of travellers, border guards, and in some case armed soldiers. There was no standing in line and shuffling forward one at a time between neat little roped off lanes. It was a melee of 40 or 50 passengers mixed in with uniformed custom and immigration officials packed into one room. In order for the border guards to know who had been searched and who hadn't, they placed a chalk mark on the outside of luggage that had been searched. So when you finally managed to push your way to the door leading out to the plane, you presented your boarding pass and showed the door guard your chalked marked suitcase. That is when I started carrying some chalk with me and when no one was looking, marked my own luggage and that of any crew member close by.

Another time while en route back to the ship we had to change planes, I think it was Brazzaville in the Republic of Congo, for the flight out to the coast. Most of our flights into west Africa started out in either London or Paris, landing in a major city or hub. We were then transferred to smaller local airlines for the final leg of our journey. After the Paris or London flight had landed, we were all herded into a room to await the flight to our final destination. This room, and the various parts of the airport we passed through were all covered completely in white tiles, floors, walls, and ceilings. It was almost like a sterile hospital setting. The room we were escorted into was nothing but white tiles covering every surface, no seats, no windows, nothing. We were told to remain in this room and not leave until our flight was called. At this time there was a lot of fighting between the Congo and Angola, so the airport was crawling with heavily armed soldiers. In fact, our escorts to the white room were also armed to the teeth soldiers, but there was a problem, I had to pee. I held it as long as I could, but finally decided I had to go in search of a mens room. After leaving the white room I spotted a sign for the mens room just a short distance across the corridor. However, I was stopped in my tracks by a huge pool of blood just outside the entrance to the washroom. Leading from the pool of blood were two parallel lines of blood leading directly into the washroom. It looked like someone had dragged a bleeding body across the floor and into said washroom. All of a sudden the need to pee had mysteriously vanished and I scurried back to the white room.

And lastly the case of the humorous sweat shirt. While tied up in Den Helder one of the crew came back aboard wearing a new and very nice sweat shirt. Across the front of this shirt were a series of about six embroidered signal flags. Before the advent of radio for communication between ships, flag hoists were used. Every ship is required to carry a set of these signal flags. There are 26 alphabet flags, 10 number flags, and 4 substitute flags. Each letter flag has a specific meaning when flown separately. The A flag means I have a diver down, the B flag means I am carrying dangerous goods, the C flag means I have a pilot on board, the Q flag means my vessel is healthy and I request free pratique, and so on. You can also group several flags together in the form of a code as laid out in the International Code of Signals publication. The four flags I just mentioned are the more common ones in use today. If you see a grouping of flags you can go to the Code of Signals publication to decipher its meaning. There are several sections in this book, such as general signals, distress and emergency signals, and one for medical signals. As soon as I saw this guys sweat shirt I wanted to know if this flag grouping had a particular meaning. I thumbed through the various sections looking to see if the flags displayed on his shirt had a specific meaning or were they just a random group of colourful flags. I finally found it in the medical section. That particular grouping of flags translated to, the patient has discharge from his penis. Someone had a good sense of humour!

CHAPTER 13

BC FERRY CORPORATION

A<small>FTER RETURNING HOME FROM MY LAST</small> trip aboard the ill-fated Probe researcher, I was now unemployed. It had always been my intention, while working offshore, of securing a position with a company that offered benefits, especially a pension plan. The only two choices I could see were coastal tugs such as Seaspan, or BC Ferries. I therefore drafted a resume which included all my sea time, experiences, and qualifications. I then mailed it off to the various tug boat firms and to BC Ferries. I got zero responses. At this time there happened to be more qualified ships officers on the beach than there were positions for them to fill. I also did not know of BC Ferries hiring practices. It turned out they would only hire ships officers from within. If you were already working for them in some other capacity, a deck hand or a parking lot attendant, and a posting came up for a licensed officer you could apply for it. A practice that has come back to haunt them in todays world. I was not too worried though, I had only been home a short while. It was summer, and I had enough money, especially with Louise working, to last me for awhile.

Around September of that year, 1989, I got a break. I was talking to a fellow from the Nanaimo Yacht Club I knew, who had worked for the ferries. I remember it clearly, we were standing in the Nanaimo Yacht Club parking lot, it was a beautiful warm sunny day, and I was questioning him about working for the ferries and how one goes about getting hired. This is when he explained their hiring practices. The idea was to get hired as an, on call casual, which then gives you the right to apply for a posted position. He also told me if I was serious, drive up to Comox and go see a guy named Blake. I drove up that very afternoon, knocked on Blakes door and was hired on the spot.

For the next year, or so, I worked as either chief officer or captain on all the northern Gulf Island ferries from Gabriola Island to Alert Bay, including the Texeda Island ferry. Because I was on call I was required to carry a pager, no cell phones yet. If I missed three calls in a row, or turned down three calls, then I would be terminated. Most of these small ferries had a six days on three days off rotation. However, in order for management to deny me time off, they would assign me to a ferry for only five days and then immediately transfer me to another ferry. No time off. Comox was my home base so I would get travel expenses, meals and mileage, from Comox to whatever ferry I was posted to, despite the fact that I lived in Vancouver at the time. However, now that I was a player in the game I could apply for any job posting throughout the entire fleet.

I must have applied for several posting a week, but because I had almost zero seniority, it was going to take some time. I finally got my chance when I applied for a masters posting for the MV Kuna, a small ferry that runs between Graham Island and Moresby Island in the Queen Charlottes Islands. The reason I won that posting was that no one else wanted to move to the Charlottes. The crew rotation was two weeks on and one week off, which gave me a chance to fly home, at my own expense, for my week off. I also had to supply my own accommodation, which took the form of borrowing my parents travel trailer and shipping it aboard the Queen of Prince Rupert from Port Hardy to Skidegate. Once it was offloaded in Skidegate, I borrowed the company truck, with out asking for permission, to move it via the Kuna over to Alliford Bay. I figured if there was any flack to come my way for the use of the truck, it was better to beg for forgiveness than be denied its use in the first place. I then parked it in a trailer park of sorts next to the ferry landing. Before BC Ferries took over the running of the Kuna, it and all the gulf Island ferries, were managed by the Department of Highways. All these small ferries tied up for the night on the islands they serviced. Since accommodation for the casual crews was sparse or non existent, the Highways maintained a mobile home style of bunkhouse on each island. In the case of the Alliford Bay ferry, not only was there this bunk house but three or four serviced RV pads as well. It was a strange situation, no one seemed to know who owned the property, which didn't stop the ferries from making use of the bunk house and allowing people, like myself, to park and live in an RV on the site. I did have to pay for hydro though, to a squatter who was living in a tar paper shack down the hill from the site and who had tapped into one of the serviced pads.

While working on the Kuna, I learned that the Queen of Prince Rupert, which ran between Prince Rupert and Skidegate for the summer months only, would hire temporary crews from around the fleet. The crew rotation was two weeks on and two weeks off, better than the Kuna. Plus it was a real ship with a live aboard crew. So I applied and was hired for the summer as chief officer. I did two summers with the Queen of Prince Rupert, with the winters spent back with the Kuna. Around that time I decided to make the move south to a ferry closer to home. Accordingly, I accepted a chief officers position on SaltSpring Island aboard one of the original ferries, the Queen of Nanaimo, which ran between Long Harbour on Saltspring Island and Tsawwasen with stops at Pender Island, Maine Island and Galiano Island. This was OK except for the fact that as chief officer I was responsible for loading and unloading the car deck. A glorified over qualified parking lot attendant. I don't recall how long I stayed with the Saltspring Island ferry but eventually I moved to the Queen of Alberni out of Departure Bay, again as a well paid parking lot attendant. While working on the Alberni, a permanent posting for chief officer northern came available, which I applied for and won. I was now chief officer for the Queen of Prince Rupert and the Queen of the North. This is what I had been waiting for, no more days spent loading cars and trucks. The chief officer northern was expected to man the bridge and assume the duties of a navigator. On top of this I was expected to be able to relieve as master should the need arise. As it turned out I sailed as master about 80% of the time. There was one year I recall where I served as captain for that entire year.

    That about wraps up my journey. I enjoyed my time aboard both the Queen of Prince Rupert and the Queen of the North for many reasons. When working as chief officer I loved navigating up and down the coast from Port Hardy to Prince Rupert and from Prince Rupert to the Queen Charlotte Islands. On sunny summer days this was a walk in the park. However, in the winter months with the storms bringing high winds, driving rain, sleet or snow, this could be a challenge. I also, when working as master, loved the ship handling aspect of the job. Again, under some very trying weather conditions. Finally, I loved the live aboard life style. When living and working on a ship for extended periods, you develop a bond with the rest of the crew. Sort of like a family. It is a completely different situation with the back-and-forth daily routine of the ferries that sail between the mainland and Vancouver Island. These routes are day jobs, where you work for an eight-hour day and then go home for the night. There is very little interaction between crew members. I always compared it to driving a taxi for an eight-hour shift.

I retired in early 2006 about two months before the Queen of the North met her untimely end or I would have been her captain on that fateful night. There was a Queen of the North reunion party that same year. I met and talked with many of the crew members I had worked with over the years that were on board that night. One young lady who worked in catering told me her story. Most of the crews were housed in cabins below the water line. When the ship hit Gil Island the wardrobe in her cabin was knocked over blocking the door to her cabin and preventing her escape. The water was up to her knees when she resigned herself to her fate and simply went back to bed to await the end. Fortunately, several seaman used a fire axe to break down her door and rescue her just in time. She never went back to work for the ferries again. Many of the people at the reunion told me they wished I had been the captain that night, because the accident would never have happened. Maybe, maybe not, I was just glad I was not there to see the final moments of a beautiful ship.

After retirement, Louise and I bought a class A motorhome and spent the next 15 years driving to Mexico for the winter. We would spend 5 months in a beautiful RV park in a small town, about 55 kilometres north of Puerto Vallarta, called Lo De Marcos. It typically would take us 2 weeks to drive down and 2 weeks to drive back home. The 2 week drive down and back gave us time to visit tourist attractions along our route. My favourite sites to visit included hot springs and air museums. Louise's favourite stop was at various outlet malls. We stopped going to Mexico in 2018.

During the summer months I sail and maintained my small sailboat. The first boat I owned was a 26 foot double ended cutter designed by William Alkin around 1926. She was named Grayling. My boat was built with a fibreglass hull sometime around 1985. However, everything above the hull was wood, deck, cabin, bulwarks, etc. As a result there was lots of painting and varnishing to keep her looking good. I owned her for 35 years. Then in the summer of 2018 I stumbled across a fibreglass sailboat, called a Vancouver 27, which was up for sale in the same marina as Grayling. I had long coveted this design which were produced in Vancouver in the 1980's. At that time a complete boat would cost around $90,000.00, a huge amount of money for the 80's, money I did not have. I had to have her. She is named Elspeth, which is Scottish for Elizabeth. The problem with buying a new boat was that I first had to sell Grayling. Boats are not like cars, they can take months, even years, to sell and owning two boats at the same time was out of the question. As soon as I saw the for sale sign attached to Elspeth's life lie, I scurried over to the nearest boat broker and listed Grayling for sale. I had a buyer less than 24 hours later, it was meant to be.

With Mexico out of the picture, I was now able go to work for the Nanaimo Yacht Club dock crew. We work mostly in the fall, winter, and into the spring, with the summers off and devoted to sailing. Our work entails the repairs and maintenance of the existing docks, fingers, and boat houses. We are also involved with new construction, replacing the aging infrastructure, some of which is well past its due date.

PROLOGUE

I WAS BORN DONALD JOHN CRIGHTON on June 4, 1946, the oldest of three children, in Vancouver, British Columbia, Canada. Growing up in the Vancouver area I was surrounded by the ocean. As children we would spend our summer days at one of the local beaches and eventually the month of August at Crescent Beach, a small seaside resort community of summer cottages. I'm sure the close proximity to so much water, the ocean as well as the many lakes and rivers, probably had something to do with my fascination of all things water related. I learned to swim at an early age and still do as often as possible. I also became an avid scuba diver, only giving it up when I turned 75 years young. It must go without saying, I was in love with boats of every description, starting off with a small runabout and finally graduating to a sailboat.

I also had a fascination with the navy and as a result joined the Royal Canadian Navy Reserve at the age of 16. We would meet every Tuesday night at HMCS Discovery, a base in Vancouver harbour, where for several hours a night we would practice marching around in formation. We would also receive instruction in one of several fields of our choosing. I chose to be a stores-man. We only had three choses from which to choose, the other two being, a medic or a signalman. I get queasy just looking at blood and I didn't think I could learn morse code, so "Victualling Stores", it was. We also trained with several fire arms, an FN rifle, a

9mm pistol, and a Sten gun. My group of fellow marchers would participate in several Vancouver parades through out the year, May Day, Remembrance Day, and such. Sometimes we would be required to give a 3 or 7 gun salute with our FN rifles, like the spring opening of the Royal Vancouver Yacht, for example. We would also spend one month each summer with the regular navy at a base or ship somewhere in Canada. My summers were spent mostly at HMCS Naden in Victoria. I stayed with the reserves until I was 21 years old, rising from the rank of Ordinary Seaman through Able Seaman and finally Leading Seaman.

After high school it was expected that I attend university. This turned out to be a dismal failure. I had no ambition, no goals, and I could not wrap my head around studying for four years to achieve nothing but a piece of paper. I was not a good student. What to do? I quit university and took off for a back packing trip around Europe. Myself and my two friends bought a Volkswagen van in Frankfurt Germany. We travelled through out Europe, making it as far south as Morocco, finally ending up in Switzerland. In the small Swiss village of Leysin, we got jobs working for the local ski resort as lift operators and occasional ski patrol. When the ski season ended I said goodbye to my two travelling companions and headed for London England. In London I purchased a new BSA 650 motorcycle. I first toured around England before taking the hovercraft back to Europe. I rode as far south as Greece and as far north as Norway. I then headed for Hamburg Germany where I booked passage for myself and my motorcycle on a passenger carrying cargo ship bound for New York. From New York I travelled north into Quebec and then west all the way back to Vancouver.

After arriving back in Vancouver, the first thing I did was to reconnect with, Louise, my girl friend and future wife.

Together we made plans to earn enough money in order for us to return to Leysin for the next winters ski season, where my job as lift operator was waiting for me. We were living together, but not married, something both of our parents objected to. In order to convince us that getting married was a good idea, they promised us return airfare to Switzerland as a wedding gift. We agreed. I returned to my old job and Louise found work in a small hotel as a chambermaid. It was a wonderful winter. However, after returning home to Vancouver it was time to think about settling down and finding a good job to support us both. That is when I got my first paying sea going job with the Canadian Coast Guard.

I can't recall how long I worked for the Coast Guard, maybe a couple of years. One of the coxswains I worked with was an English sailor who had survived the sinking of six ships during WW 2. After the war he immigrated to Canada and became a commercial salmon fisherman. I loved to hear his stories from the war as well as his days of fishing the West Coast of Vancouver Island. In fact, he still owned a small fishing boat which was up for sale. Say no more. I purchased that boat, quit the coast guard and embarked on a new career as a commercial fisherman. In my six or seven years as a fisherman I owned three different boats, all relatively small salmon trollers, but in those days the future of the industry was seen to be larger boats with on board refrigeration in order to freeze the catch within hours of being caught. I had arranged to buy such a boat during the course of my last season. At the seasons end and after selling my last boat, I approached the owner of the boat I had arranged to buy, cheque in hand. He, however, had changed his mind and refused to sell the boat. That final season for me, and every other fisherman on the coast, had been a banner year. The fish were plentiful and the price of fish was at a record high. As a result no one wanted to sell a boat when everyone was making money hand over fist. I should add that it wasn't just a boat I was buying, but also the salmon license that came with it. The only way to get a salmon license was to buy an already existing one as the Department of Fisheries had stopped issuing licenses many many years before I came upon the scene. So no boat, effectively ending my career as a commercial fisherman. Actually, I was very lucky. That banner year was the last of its kind. The following years went from bad to worst, dwindling fish stocks, lower prices for fish, and new restrictive government regulations all conspired to make it more and more difficult to earn a living as a commercial fisherman. Several of my friends were forced to declare bankruptcy, loosing everything including their homes.

With my career as a commercial fisherman coming to an abrupt end, I now had to decide on my next step. I had long envisioned going back to school and studying for the Canadian Department of Transport, Certificates of Competency. These certificates or tickets are needed in order to find employment as a ship's officer. The starting point was a third mates certificate, called a Watch Keeping Mates Certificate. This particular ticket is the basic building block upon which all future tickets are built. There are a variety of routes to take to climb the ship's officer ladder, such as inland tickets, minor waters tickets, and coastal or home trade tickets. In my mind the Holy Grail of certificates is an ocean going ticket, known as foreign going. This would allow me to sail on any ship the world over, as opposed to being restricted to the West Coast, the Fraser River, or some inland lake. It is also the longest route to take, requiring more sea time, more schooling, and more exams to be written and passed. Speaking of sea time, this is a requirement to even apply for admittance to the watch keeping mates course. Sea time, literally time at sea, is also required between each rung of the ticket ladder. I needed two years of sea time before I could approach Camosun College in Victoria and make application to study for this first basic ticket. Fortunately, I found I could use my time as a commercial fisherman for this requirement. After achieving the third mate's certificate, I would need another year of sea time, sailing as a third mate, before I could write for my second mate's certificate. Likewise, going from second mate to chief mate would require another years sea time, that is 365, eight hour days of working at sea, and finally, one more year of sea time to go from chief mate to master mariner.

The first step was to have my sea time approved by the coast guard. I was then able to enrol in the six month long watch keeping mate's course at Cameron College in Victoria BC. The course went smoothly, and after passing all my exams and a final oral exam with the coast guard examiner, I was issued my first certificate. I also learned all about the Canadian system of certificates of competency. Camosun College played no roll in issuing theses certificates, they only prepared the student to sit for the exams, which were all prepared, written, and marked by the coast guard examiners. Anyone, with the required sea time, could walk into the coast guard office, pay a small fee and book an exam. Once I learned this important fact, I was able to study on my own at my own pace and book an exam whenever I felt ready. This system worked well for me, verses structured courses of study, whether at Camosun College, or the Pacific Marine Training Institute, PMTI, in Vancouver. These structured courses were geared to the slowest learner, which I didn't have time for. As a university student, I was a complete flop, but as an aspiring ship's officer I went to the head of the class. I now had ambition and a goal and I was off and running. Whenever I had a month off, I would pay a library fee at PMTI and study ten hours a day. This fee gave me a cubicle in the library, access to all the books and publications in the library, and the right to query any instructor in the school, should I need a question answered. In this way way I completed my next ticket, called ON2, second mate foreign going, in only two months. The same system applied to the following tickets, the ON1, chief mate foreign going, and finally Master Mariner, master foreign going. If I had to take time off from work and signed up for these six month long courses, it would have taken me twice or even three times as long to attain my goal of earning my Master Mariners Certificate. Also working in my favour was the fact that most of my jobs required me to work 12 hour days, which meant for every day worked I collected a day and a half of sea time. I did the entire thing from start to finish in only six years, which I believe is a record.

I had many wonderful jobs over the years, starting with the MV Western Hemlock as third mate. I was also able to visit countries and ports all over the world, places few tourist ever see or would want to. The only draw back for me, were the long overseas airline flights. I disliked these flights so much that on one occasion I came close to walking off a Lufthansa flight from Vancouver to Frankfurt. I was seated next to a lady with an attitude. When I opened the overhead bin in order to stow my carry-on I found she had laid her coat over the entire bottom of the bin. Not wanting to put my bag on top of the coat I carefully folded it in half and placed my bag in the empty half of the bin. The lady saw what I was doing and exploded, "I touched her valuable coat, I creased the coat, how dare I put my luggage in her bin", and on and on. When I tried to sit down next to her she was off again, "I'm not sitting next to you, you'll have to find another seat". The stewardesses quickly rushed over to try and defuse the situation but the lady refused to sit next to me. For the next several minutes I watched as they walked her up and down the aisle, trying to find a suitable seat she would be happy with. The seat I was in was at the rear of the plane right next to the galley, and because I did not escalate the situation by getting angry or even raising my voice, the stewardesses plied me food and drink the entire flight.

So, let the adventure begin.

As with all true stories, I have changed the names of anyone mentioned in order to protect the guilty.

APPENDIX A

CELESTIAL NAVIGATION

CELESTIAL NAVIGATION, OR ASTRONAVIGATION, IS A method of fixing a vessels position when out of sight of land. It uses a sextant to measure the angle of a celestial body, the sun, moon, or stars, above the horizon and then using tables or mathematical formulas to solve a spherical triangle. There are several ways to ascertain the ships position with the use of a sextant, one being the altitude intercept method, also called the Marcq St. Hiliare method, after the Frenchman who first invented it. This is the method I was first taught and used through out my career. I won't go into the mathematics behind this method as they are way too complicated even for the navigator who is employing it at sea. Taking a sight of the sun during the day is fairly simple and straightforward. After determining the angle of the sun above the horizon, the navigator then uses this number to calculate a line of position or LOP. This not a fix as the ship maybe anywhere on that line. The next step is to take at least three sights of the sun spaced an hour or more apart. Waiting an hour between each sight means your LOPs will be at an angle to each other. When the sun is at its highest position in the sky, local noon, the line of position becomes your latitude. The navigator then advances his three morning LOPs using the ships course and speed until they all meet the latitude at, hopefully, a single point. Where these LOPs all cross is the vessels noon position.

The stars are also used in this way, but with the advantage of ascertaining the vessels actual position within a few minutes. When taking star sights the navigator must have everything planned in advance. This is because you must be able to see the stars and the horizon at the same time, which can only happen for a few minutes at sundown or sunup. To begin my preparations for taking these sights I would select three or four stars I new would be in the sky at the time of the ships approximate position. I also needed to select stars that were separated in azimuth by as many degrees as possible, that is one star looking north, one looking east, one looking south and one looking west. If you select stars that are too close together in the night sky then your LOP's, when plotted on the chart, are almost parallel to each other and will not cross each other. With the help of tables, I would pre-plot each stars azimuth and elevation for the estimated time of taking the sights. Then I would pre-set the sextant for the estimated elevation, stand next to the bridge wing gyro compass facing the estimated direction, acquire the star in the sextant's telescope, and adjust the sextant so that the star is just touching the horizon. After making a note of the actual elevation of the star and the exact time of the sight, I would hurriedly pre-set the sextant for the estimated elevation of my next star, rush back out onto the bridge wing, take my second star sight, and so on. After completing the three or four observations, I now had to calculate the altitude intercept for each star and then plot my LOP's on a plotting sheet. Plotting sheets are large chart size sheets of paper with only the lines of latitude printed on them. The lines of longitude are drawn in but not specified. You appoint each line of longitude a number based roughly on where the ship is positioned and in which ocean. I would normally plot my last LOP first. The first three LOP's must then be advanced to the time of the final LOP using the ship's speed and heading so that all four LOP's will have the same time stamp. Where these LOP's intersect is the position of the ship at the time of the forth or last star sight.

Manufactured by Amazon.ca
Acheson, AB